A SEASON IN VAIL

ALSO BY STEVE BASKA

50 Questions for Thinking Christians
(2017, Jayhawk Mountain Press)

A SEASON IN VAIL

HE CAME TO SKI AND DISCOVERED MORE

a novel

STEVE BASKA

A SEASON IN VAIL

978-0-9989974-2-1 (Paperback)
978-0-9989974-3-8 (eBook)

This is a work of fiction. The persons are imagined. Any resemblance to persons, live or dead, is purely coincidental.

Published in the United States
by Jayhawk Mountain Press, Castle Pines, Colorado

DEDICATION

This book is dedicated to all skiers and snowboarders who ride the white carpet in resorts across the world, and especially to the men and women who founded and work in the Vail, Colorado ski resort and town. I would also like to thank the following friends: brothers Scott Baska and Lee Green for writing encouragement; wife Vickie for daily love and support; and Doug Moen and Stephanie Moen for input and text review, and book producer David Wogahn for his good guidance and support through the publishing process.

Go confidently in the direction of your dreams.
Live the life you have imagined.

—Henry David Thoreau

CONTENTS

AUTHOR'S NOTE:

Snow skiing is a sport and a culture. While this novel is set in Vail, Colorado, I've also tried to capture a bit of the wider story of the sport and its people and varied places. Readers should know that this novel includes two different types of information: real, non-fiction history and details of Vail and the sport, and a fictional story of a man who moves to Vail to become a ski instructor. None of the characters in this book are real people, but the places they go in Colorado and the town of Vail are real. This style, sometimes called "realistic fiction," has been used by many writers who have placed fictional characters in real towns, wars, and historic situations. I recommend that readers see the Chapter Notes section in back of the book for sources where real information was publicly reported.

I lived in Vail, Colorado for one winter season (1978-79), when I was 22, after I graduated from college at Kansas University and before I began a career as a newspaper reporter covering city governments, politics and business. A college friend of mine had lived in Vail the previous winter and found it a rewarding experience, so I was eager to live the ski life for one season. I lived in a small condominium in west Vail with two other young men and worked the first half the season at the Gorsuch ski shop in Vail Village and the second half as a grill cook at the Eagles Nest restaurant on top of the mountain above Lionshead. I made friends with all kinds of locals, from ski instructors to the owner of the Vail newspaper. Vail was a magical place to me and I mean to honor it in this book. To research this book I interviewed current and former ski instructors and patrollers from Vail and other areas, and Vail Valley locals. I also did extensive research on the Internet for ski and Vail issues. Those websites are cited where appropriate.

1

WINTER SEASON STARTS WITH A BANG

Beware of missing chances, otherwise it may
be altogether too late someday.
—Franz Liszt

On the first of December a morning snow fell and swirled in a circle dance across Vail mountain and much of Colorado. It was the first heavy snowfall of the winter season, and as the sun climbed over the ridges, ski instructors and patrollers gathered their equipment and began making their way to the chairlifts and gondolas. It was good to see the white gold finally falling heavy for it meant their way of life was coming in to settle after too little of the frozen water had dropped in November. But it was here now. The ski life. The mountain life. Riders of the white frosting all across the valley pulled open the curtains of their bedrooms and took in the scene with gladness.

In a few minutes, lift operators were at their posts waking up the beast of many chairs. The chairlifts groaned and began to move. The lifties stood with brooms and swept snow off each chair that would carry precious lives high above the ground. The instructors and patrollers soon rode to the top and began to take the first runs of the day, well before the chairs opened to the public. A cold wind bit at their necks as they carved left and right, sometimes in pairs, watching the tips of their skis and snowboards nose forward into the fresh unbroken powder. And as they looked over the awakening valley, a passing mountain lion looked down on the skiers from higher yet and continued her silent walk through trees in hopes of finding a herd of elk she knew lived in this valley.

A few hours later and eight hundred miles to the west in sunny Los Angeles, attorney Tom Woods sat at the defense table and adjusted his tie and looked through his notes as he prepared to present his summation to the jury. His teenage client squirmed in the seat beside Tom and asked when the judge would arrive.

"Any moment now," Tom said. The end of this murder trial could not come soon enough for Tom. It had been a long hard grind to defend this college boy of a rich family who had allegedly assaulted a girl at a party before she jumped from a rooftop to her death.

The judge arrived and banged his gavel and looked over glasses that sat on the end of his nose.

"Good morning," the judge said. "Are we ready for summations?"

Tom nodded yes. The prosecutor nodded yes.

"Okay, Mr. Woods. Let's hear the defense comments first, shall we?" the judge said. Tom looked at his client, Billy Sawtell, the likely heir to his father's real estate fortune, or at least the likely heir until now. Tom was sure they would lose this case and Billy would spend his remaining hormone-fueled years in prison. Billy had been a terrible client: he had lied to the police, and his smug grin and entitled attitude were evident to the jury every day that he appeared in court. Tom felt sure the jury would convict him without hesitation.

Tom rose and walked to the jury box. "Ladies and gentlemen, Billy Sawtell is no saint, but this girl's death was not his fault," he said. "As you have heard, they were both intoxicated and alone in his room. Billy claims their relations were consensual and there is no witness to dispute it. When the victim Julie Porter went out the window and stood on the ledge, it was her own choice. My client should not be convicted for her poor choice and her tragic fall. I urge you to see the circumstances and reasonable doubt that exist in this case."

As Tom said down, the prosecutor rose and approached the jury box. "That's a nice story, but it does not fit the facts we've heard. On the ledge, Julie Porter screamed at the defendant to not come near her. Two witnesses say she claimed, while on the ledge, that Billy raped her and she would not let him touch her again. She backed away as he reached for her and she fell. Billy Sawtell caused this death as surely as if he had pushed her. "

As the judge sent the jury out to deliberate, Billy was taken back to his cell and Tom went to the cafeteria with Billy's parents.

"How does it look?" the father asked.

"The witnesses' comments and the bruises on her neck are quite damaging," Tom said.

"I'm not paying you for negativity," the father said.

"We need to be realistic."

After an hour, the court clerk came to Tom and said the jury is coming back in. Billy and the spectators and the media moved back in the courtroom.

"Mister foreman," the judge said. "What say you on the charges?"

"On the charge of rape, guilty. On the charge of negligent homicide, guilty."

Billy looked blank for a moment, then screamed toward the judge.

"She wanted to do it. I did not push her over the railing. This is not fair," he said. Then Billy made a run for the door and was tackled by a guard. Billy reached for the guard's gun and pulled it from the holster. The guard grabbed Billy's arm, but Billy's hand waved free with the gun and he began pulling the trigger. Three loud pops echoed in the small courtroom. A shot hit the ceiling, another hit a wall and a third plowed into Tom Woods' briefcase that Tom held up in front of himself.

· · · · · · ·

Billy was hauled away screaming. Tom looked at his briefcase with a hole in it. He opened the case and pulled out a thick book that had the bullet lodged in the middle of it. He pulled the bullet out and held it up and looked at it, then sat down and wiped his forehead. His co-counsel, Edward Anderson, said "That was close. Are you okay?" Tom felt over his body for sign of injury. "Yes, I appear to be okay."

Billy's father came over to Tom and said "You were supposed to be the best defense attorney in LA. I guess that is not true."

Tom stared in amazement at the man and said "Thanks for your words of concern after your son almost shot me."

Tom regained his composure and went out into the hallway where TV reporters and cameramen had gathered to wait for comments by the parties. The combination of the murder, the topic of student rape and defendant being son of a well-known local citizen had kept the trial in the news. The reporters shouted questions at Tom. "Your client went wild. What happens now?"

"We'll have to see," Tom said.

Will you appeal the verdict?

"We'll have to see. I'll have some comment later."

Tom and Edward drove back to their office on the 20th floor of a Los Angeles downtown building. Tom's assistant jumped up from her desk and said "I heard it on the news. Are you okay?" Tom nodded and waved off her concern. He headed to his glass-paneled office, which had his name neatly etched into the glass door: Thomas Woods IV. As he slammed his briefcase down on this desk, his father came walking in quickly.

"Son, are you okay?," said his father, who founded their firm of Woods, Mason and Johnson.

"Yes, damn it. I told you the kid was crazy. He has that look in his eyes, and the attitude. I knew this was possible."

"I know, but you did your best and we had to represent him. His father is too big a client to refuse."

"His father is crazy too. I'm done with this case. Put somebody else on it."

When his father left, Tom shut his door and looked at the collage of photographs on one of his walls. Some showed him at law school graduation, on the beach in the south of France, on the ski slopes of Aspen and Vail, and working in a village in Africa digging water wells.

His co-counsel on this case, Edward, came in to Tom's office. Tom and Edward were almost identical in appearance and career: mid-thirties, short dark hair, square jawed handsome faces, tailored suits and quick minds all helped their career ascent in the office.

Edward said "Hey, hot shot, everybody loses a case occasionally. Shake it off."

Tom held up the bullet. "What do you think that is? A 45? A 9 millimeter?

"Who cares? It didn't have your name on it, so take the day off and clear your head."

Tom stood in front of his photo wall again. "Did you ever think of doing anything besides the law?" he asked.

"No. I like it. I mean except when the hand guns come out."

Tom stared back at the photos.

"Oh, don't tell me," Edward said. "You're going to Africa again. You're tired of the law. Ten years of criminal defense work is your max and now you're out."

"I still like the law. I'm just thinking of options."

"Oh, that's how it starts. The options. Well, God knows you've got them. Millions in the bank already. A golden touch with stock trading that you could do from anywhere in the world and just keep getting richer. And single. You do know I hate you, right?"

Tom waved a dismissive hand gesture at his friend. Tom's assistant buzzed his desk phone: "Christine on line two, Mr. Woods."

Edward rolled his eyes and left the room. Tom punched the speaker button on the phone and said hello.

"Hi honey" said the high thin voice on the line. "I saw you on TV and about the shooting. Thomas, are you okay?

"Don't call me Thomas, and yes I'm fine."

"Okay, then. Can we eat at La Scala tonight?"

Tom held out the phone in front of him and then banged it gently on his forehead. His near-miss at being shot had barely registered one moment of empathy with his girlfriend before her thoughts turned back to her own desire for dinner in Beverly Hills. I've got to rethink this girl, he thought. Sure, she was beautiful and interested in art like he was, but where was the emotional intelligence?

"Sure," he said. "You make the reservation and tell me when to pick you up."

"Okay, honey. I'll call you back," she said.

That night at dinner Tom sat between his girlfriend and his father, a barrel-chested man of 65, sharp of wit and kind of heart. His father, whom everyone called by his middle name, Scott, had made his money first in commercial real estate before attending law school and founding a small law firm that grew into one of the most prestigious firms in the city.

"Son, I am so sorry about today," his father said. "We should never have to be in danger like that."

"It's made me stop and think," Tom said.

Tom's mother looked up from the menu. "About what, dear?"

"Perhaps it's time for a change of scenery, and work. Maybe I don't need to practice criminal law my whole life."

His mother, Iris, frowned. "What would you do?" she said. "Not that Africa water well volunteer thing again."

Christine frowned and said "Tom, what are you talking about?" And then without skipping a beat she said "You know, we should have our wedding reception here."

"I have not asked you to marry me yet," Tom said.

"Oh, fiddle," Christine said. "Just details."

"What if I said...," Tom paused long, "...that I was moving to Colorado this winter."

His parents and girlfriend looked at him and frowned.

"Oh. My. Gosh," the girlfriend said. "You are such a kidder. There's nothing in Colorado but rocks. Except at Aspen, of course."

Tom's father looked over his glasses that sat on the end of his nose and said "He's not kidding. I know my boy. Where?"

"Vail," Tom said.

Tom's mother said "Aspen's little brother? Oh, my gosh. Scott, our boy is going to become a ski bum. What will our friends say? "

Tom smiled. He had been through this before, with Africa and other travels. He loved his parents, but now at 36, he felt totally independent of their opinions, demands and manipulations. He was prepared to let their comments wash over him and slide down onto the floor, swirling like water into a puddle at his feet.

"Son, you know I want you to take over the firm someday," his father said.

"All options are open, dad."

Tom's mother fanned herself. Christine's mouth dropped open.

Christine said "I am not moving to some God-forsaken mountain town just because you like to ski."

"I'm not asking you to," Tom said. He held back a smile. He felt he had seen Christine clearly for the first time, and all he could think of was a mannequin in a store window: Perfect face, a neck draped in diamonds, perfect dress and body shaped down to the toes, and not a single generous thought for anyone else inside that beautiful frame.

She started to cry and said "Everything was okay yesterday."

Tom's mother jumped in to smooth things over. "It's like that song about yesterday by that nice boy in the Beatles band, Pat McCarthy," she said. "I think he wrote that other song too, Eleanor Grigsby. I had a friend in high school named Eleanor Grigsby. Isn't that funny?"

Tom groaned and said "His name is McCartney. There's an N in the name. And it's Eleanor Rigby. Rig-bee."

"No, my friend's name was Grigsby. She was from a very good family."

Tom sat back in his chair and said "I'm sure she was."

Tom felt in his pocket and pulled out the bullet. He set it down on the table by his plate. Its tip was blunt and flattened. He planned to keep the small lump of metal for a long time.

Christine sniffled as she wiped her eyes and looked at it. "What is that thing?" she said.

"That's the bullet that nearly killed me today. I'm wondering, Christine, did that have any impact on your thinking today?"

She sneered and said nothing.

Tom's father said "Son, why don't you get away for a few days. It's December first today. Vail is probably open for skiing now."

Tom nodded and rolled the bullet around in his palm and said "Good idea, dad."

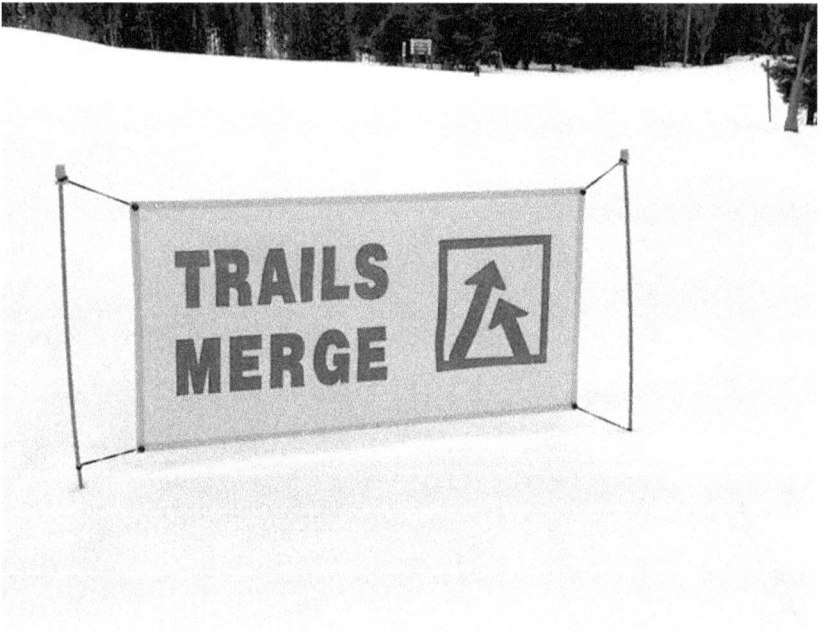

2

TO EACH HIS OWN SPORT

A man in passion rides a horse that runs away with him.
—Thomas Fuller.

Statistics show there are 125 million skiers and snowboarders worldwide in the late twenty teens. Across the globe there are 2,131 lift-served snow resorts in 66 countries. In the United States, about 9.8 million people went skiing or snowboarding in the year prior to Spring 2018, down from 11.2 million in Spring 2009. But while the ski market has slowed in some areas in recent years after the industry was born and grew fast in the middle 1900s, a passion for skiing continues around the world.

European resorts have the most visits each season in this era. Only three North American resorts made it into the top 20 most visited list, including Canada's Whistler-Blackcomb (#6), and Colorado's Vail (#9) and Breckenridge (#11).

China has had the fastest rise in attendance at ski resorts, followed by Russia, due to new ski areas built in those countries which have brought their total ski areas to 646 in China and 354 in Russia. And there are smaller countries with ski operations where many people may be surprised to find them, including Greece, India, Iran, Israel, Lebanon, Pakistan, South Africa and Turkey.

There's something about skiing and snowboarding that people love, but what is it? Some say it is the excitement of going fast and avoiding the dangers of injury. Others say it is a feeling of "dancing with the mountains," making precise steps that bring pleasure and a sense of accomplishment that you are mastering a skill. Many say it is the combination of other factors too: being outdoors in wide open spaces with beautiful views, simply gliding next to trees brings a sense of unity with nature, riding high above the ground on a chairlift is different and exciting from our everyday routines, having fun with friends in a new setting, meeting new people in conversations on a chairlift, getting exercise, wearing different and fashionable clothes, the joy of doing or watching skiers and boarders do jumps and spins in a terrain park.

But of course, some people hate the same things: they can not master the skills or equipment or cold days, they hate being outdoors and getting exercise, and sometimes are scared of heights. To each his own sport.

· · · · · · ·

Tom Woods thought of all this the morning after the shooting, when he cleared his work schedule and boarded an airplane to Denver. He planned to rent a car and drive to Vail to clear his head and think over his option of spending the winter in Colorado. He could have flown into the Eagle-Vail airport, a few miles west of Vail, which he had done before, but he wanted to do the two hour drive from Denver to see the sights of that route. He landed at Denver International Airport and rented a BMW and soon he was on Interstate 70 going west into the foothills.

First he saw the road signs to exit for Red Rocks amphitheater, where concerts are held outside with the crowd seating between two massive red stones thrust up from the earth. He drove past the signs into the rising hills that quickly gave way to green-meadowed mountains with waves of homes perched on the hillsides and mountaintops where light snow tipped the peaks. On his left he saw a familiar house he'd seen in a Woody Allen movie called "Sleeper" and knew it was outside Denver: the white, clamshell-shaped house sat on a pedestal near the top of on the mountain close to the highway. Tom remembered Woody Allen costumed like a robot and bumping into things inside and outside that house.

In a few minutes he passed the village of Georgetown, where a long narrow lake ran beside the highway and next to the town, where thousands of mines were dug in the surrounding mountains after silver was found nearby in the late 1800s. The town was also the location of filming for several movies, including a 1978 movie "Every Which Way But Loose" starring Clint Eastwood, and a 1986 TV movie "The Christmas Gift," starring John Denver.

In a few minutes more, driving steadily uphill Tom came to the Continental Divide, the spine of the Rockies where water flows to the east on one side and to the west on the other. At this spot on I-70, he saw the ski area called Loveland right beside the road, with its carved ski runs coming down to the roadside. He saw skiers and snowboarders making turns, and people riding up the chairlifts. He passed the Loveland ski area and continued driving straight through the long Eisenhower-Johnson tunnel that cuts through the mountains right under the Continental Divide. It was dark inside and he turned on his headlights. As he drove out of the darkness and into the bright light, he drove down the west side of the Divide and into the town of Dillon, a county hub with highway exits that lead to nearby Breckenridge, Keystone, Copper Mountain and Arapahoe Basin ski areas.

These are some of the best ski areas in the world, all within a few miles, he thought. He pulled in to a gas station in Dillon and got a drink and searched on his cell phone for how many ski areas there are in Colorado.

"Twenty six," he said aloud and kept reading. He learned about the two major types of ski resorts in the world today: the luxury resorts with the biggest mountains with huge numbers of runs, hundreds of lodges and shops at the bottom of these mountains, and high prices for lift tickets well above $100 a day in America. Then there are the smaller and less expensive resorts, often called family resorts, sometimes with no night lodging or glitzy shops at the base at all, and with lifts that run slower than the luxury resorts, but full of good ski runs for tourists willing to try a more modest experience. Tom read there are at least eight such resorts in Colorado, including Eldora near Boulder, Ski Cooper near Vail, and Sunlight near Aspen.

Tom got back in his car and kept driving west and in few minutes passed the Copper Mountain ski area and then climbed over Vail Pass, just east of Vail, a high plateau area where snowmobilers and cross-country skiers had already made visible trails in the snow that day. As he descended into the Vail Valley the mountain walls were steep and he looked to his left and saw a long waterfall frozen solid, and he remembered he had read it was called "The Fang" by ice climbers who scaled the tooth-looking structure, but there were no climbers on it today.

A minute later he was passing the Vail Golf Course on this left, and then homes and condos clustering on both sides of the highway. After passing steep mountain walls of East Vail, the more gently sloping Vail mountain came quickly into view on the left of the road and the resort's ski runs gleamed with new snow on them. The moving chairlifts and gondolas and people skiing down were a welcome sight to Tom, and served as effective advertising to pull travelers off the highway. He liked that about Vail: it was a tight valley ringed by peaks, with the highway running through it. You did not have to drive miles from the highway to get to it as some resorts required.

He pulled off main exit to central Vail and in a few minutes was checking into the Sonnenalp hotel, a Swiss chalet style hotel that fit with Vail's architectural theme of a European village.

A hotel clerk welcomed him and said "Mr. Woods, it's only noon but we do have your suite ready. It has a fireplace. Would you like to schedule a massage or manicure at our spa, or take a yoga class on-site?"

"Not right now."

"Please be sure to enjoy a cocktail at our King's Club bar and our live entertainment."

"I surely will."

Tom was more in the mood to get right on the mountain. He went to his room and changed into his ski clothes and looked at his ski boots, which he had brought because he wanted his own perfect fit. He grabbed his boot bag and then walked down into Vail Village and into a ski rental shop. He asked the clerk for some demo fat skis to rent for three days.

A technician set him up with wide, flexible skis and within minutes Tom carried them to the ticket window to get a lift ticket to ride up the mountain. He asked for the price of a one full day ticket.

"$175," said the ticket seller behind the window.

Tom grimaced.

"Yep, welcome to the late twenty teens of skiing in America," the seller said. "If you had a time machine you could come back here in 1962, our opening year, when a day ticket was $5. But of course then we had just one gondola, two chair lifts, eight ski instructors, and nine ski runs. We're a bit bigger now with 31 lifts and 193 runs."

Tom knew a season pass was probably a better option for him this year, so he chose the full Vail Resorts season pass of $859 that was good for any day of the ski season and was good at 45 ski resorts worldwide.

In a few minutes he had the pass and was boarding gondola number one, an enclosed heated cabin that rose quickly up the hill. Three other people sat in the cabin with him, and Tom remembered the conversation games he used to enjoy playing on chairlifts and gondolas when he skied in recent years. His favorite game was to make up a new identity. A young couple sitting next to him asked him where he was from.

"I'm from Austria," he said. "How about you?"

"We're from Denver. Just came up for the day. You don't sound Austrian," said the young man of about 25.

"I moved there a few years ago to do my residency in cardiology. I'm originally from New York."

Tom smiled at the couple. "I'm here for a conference. It's lovely in Austria. You know, the hills are alive there, the Sound of Music movie and all that."

The young man turned and began talking to his girlfriend. The other passenger, a young woman sitting directly across from Tom, looked to him to be about 30 and probably a local resident, he judged from her skis, her clothes and her demeanor. She frowned at him and said "The hills are alive? Oh, really. You're not from Austria or New York, are you? I've played this game."

Tom looked her over.

"And what game is that, young lady?" he said.

"You make up a name and place. Nobody on the lift will know the difference. You ride up with them and never see the person again. I've done it too."

"Well," Tom said, starting into a thick European accent. "I don't know vat you are talking about. I am zee cardiologist and a ski instructor from Salzburg. I loves schussing down zee slopes of Vail, so I left my practice for just one veek. My heart is in zee mountains."

The woman rolled her eyes. "Your heart, huh?"

"Ya," he said and winked at her. "My name is Franz. And vat is yours?"

She smiled and hesitated and said "Olga."

"Vell, Olga," he said. "You are a feisty one. I think vee should have a drink together tonight to discuss this. What do you say?"

She looked Tom over and said "I'm a local. I work at Pepi's Bar and Restaurant by the covered bridge. If you happen to be there for dinner, I can serve you, and if you are nice, I could even talk to you."

The gondola pulled in to its stop at the Mid-Vail building, half way up the mountain, and they all unloaded. He turned to the girl and said "I, Franz, vill see you tonight." She rolled her eyes again and put on her skis and skied off down the mountain.

Tom looked around him. The sky was a brilliant blue, the snow was heavy on the ground. He felt good and took chairlift 4 up to a higher point. He rode by himself and put in his earbuds and starting listening to a Wes Montgomery jazz guitar song called "Bumpin." At the top of the lift he stepped off and then stood looking at the view to the south, and his gaze rested on the Mount of the Holy Cross, where snow falls into rocky cracks that show a white shape of a Christian cross. He thought of the poem about that mountain by Henry Wadsworth Longfellow and Tom began reciting it to himself as he turned and skied down the mountain, saying "There is a mountain in the distant West, that, sun-defying, in its deep ravines, displays a cross of snow upon its side."

He turned onto an intermediate run called Expresso. For the first few turns he felt unstable, so he said a few word reminders to himself as he moved: "plant, down, edge," meaning plant the pole, bend down the knees, and turn hard on the vertical edge of the skis to drive the turn instead of skidding on the flat bottom of the ski. Remember, it's all in the legs, he said aloud to himself. Keep the upper body still. He began to absorb the turns and bumps with ease, and quickly he was floating down the run, which brought him to the same chairlift again. He swung into the single rider-only line and met a single coming in from a line on the other side and they stood together for a moment and then sat on the chairlift together as it swept up the hill. The man was older, perhaps 75.

"Lovely day, isn't it?" the man asked. "A bluebird day. Blue sky above, good snow below. Life is good."

"Yes it is," Tom said. "Are you a local?"

"Yep, 40 years in the valley."

Tom pulled up his goggles so the man could see his face. Tom said "I'm in from LA for a few days, and thinking of coming back to stay for the season, need to rent or maybe buy. What do you recommend?"

The man pulled off his sunglasses and cleaned them. He had leathery skin and many wrinkles around the eyes. "I would look down valley, west, in Avon, Eagle and Edwards, especially if you buy. You'll get a lot for your money and it's only a few minutes' drive from here. So many of us locals live there, we can't afford to live in Vail. Prices are so high and there are so many second homes in Vail that sit vacant a good part of the year, waiting for the owners to come visit. It's the resort syndrome, you know, afflicting Aspen and so many resorts where the rich buy homes, so prices keep rising, and the locals and workers have to move miles away where it is more affordable. But if you are seriously loaded and want a second or third home, Vail is a great town and mountain."

"Thanks. I will look down valley too," Tom said.

Their chair moved above a small but formidable cliff of rocks, appropriately called the Chair 4 cliff, that the most advanced skiers jump over. Tom looked down and asked the old timer: "You ever jumped this cliff?"

"When my legs were younger, a few times yes," he said. "Now the body says no. To everything a season, know what I mean?"

Tom nodded yes. He adjusted his earbuds and turned on a streaming music station to smooth jazz. The two skiers said goodbye as they got off the chair and Tom started on the way down the same run as his cell phone rang. He stopped and touched a button to answer and spoke into the microphone that hung down the earbud chord.

"Hello."

"You dog. This is Andrew." Andrew was a fellow defense lawyer on a difficult case. He described a problem and asked Tom for advice.

"Andrew, I am standing on a ski run at Vail at this moment. My advice is to check your client's cell phone signal locations at the time of the crime, and for well before and after. You may have a solid defense point there."

Tom hung up and skied on down the mountain. He did a few more runs and then at three o'clock decided to quit. He headed down the run making slow looping turns down the hill, carving from one side to the other, stopping a few times to look at the Gore mountain range. At the bottom he took off his skis and walked down Bridge Street and realized he had skipped lunch, so he stopped in at Joe's Deli, a tiny sandwich shop, where he had a turkey on gluten free bread while he watched a TV monitor overhead that ran a video of a skier jumping cliffs and carving virgin powder down a massive mountain.

Tom went back to this hotel and then at 7 o'clock walked over to Pepi's restaurant, which sits on a corner on the main street. He looked inside for the girl he had met on the gondola and did not see her, and so thought he might walk around the nearby shops for a while and come back, but then she walked around a corner and spotted him. She smiled at him and came over.

"Franz, you are here."

"Ya."

"Let me get you a table. Are you alone?"

"Totally," he said. "In every sense. Alone on this trip. Not even married."

"Really?" she said.

"Oh yes. I'm a sad citizen of Salzburg. Totally alone."

"I doubt that. You look quite content to me."

She showed him to a small table by a window that looked out over shops and people walking by. She brought him a menu.

"No need," he said. "I looked it up online already. I'll have the Hungarian Veal Goulash."

"Very well. And to drink?"

"One of your best Austrian beers. You pick one for me Olga."

"You do like to take risks, don't you?"

"Sometimes, yes."

Tom looked at the small restaurant's heavy wood mountain style and thought how he liked it, a different feel from the LA décor he was used to. Olga came back with a beer and Tom said "May I ask your real name?"

She smiled. "Eva. With a long e. Eeeva Wilson."

"Tom," he said. "Plain old Tom. Woods."

He ate dinner over the next hour, checked his cell phone for texts and news and looked at the Discover Vail application on this phone. The restaurant filled up its small front dining room and a steady stream of people walked in and out of its bar in an adjacent room. Tom walked into the bar and looked at the walls covered with signed photographs of celebrities who had been there. There were photos with messages from actor Dustin Hoffman, singers, presidents and athletes.

Eva saw him and took him over to the bar where two young women sat. Eva introduced him. One of the women said "Hi Tom, my name is Summer and this is my friend Autumn."

"It's a pleasure. Is Winter coming soon?"

"We get that a lot," Summer said. "Eva says you are quite a liar on the gondola."

Tom smiled.

"What kind of work do you do?," Summer said, as Eva stood watching for a moment.

"I'm a lawyer."

Eva nodded. "Very good, right answer," she said.

"Why is that?," he said.

Summer said "Because we looked you up on the Web a minute ago. A defense lawyer from Los Angeles, and quite successful. College at Stanford."

"Well, I looked up Eva also," Tom said. "No public information on social media."

Eva shrugged her shoulders. "You can't be too careful these days about strange men from Austria poking around for information."

They all laughed and Eva went back to work and Tom drank with the two ladies. After a few minutes Eva returned and Tom said "It's been a pleasure talking with you ladies. I must be going. Eva, would you consider skiing a few runs with me tomorrow afternoon, if you are free? I am meeting a Realtor in the morning, but I'll be free by 1 p.m. Could we meet at gondola one?"

"I could be persuaded," she said. "See you then."

THIS IS THE PLACE

PETE SEIBERT'S DREAM

As a young New England skier, a combat-wounded 10th Mountain Division sergeant in World War II, then a ski patrolman, ski instructor and world-class ski racer, Pete Seibert had always dreamed of creating his own ski resort. When, in 1957, his friend Earl Eaton, an Eagle Valley native, showed him this place, now known as Vail, Pete knew he had found his dream mountain.

Working with a small group of skier-investors, Pete led his team through the acquisition of the Forest Service permit, purchase of valley land, initial financing, mountain and village design, and, finally, construction of the resort's Phase One in 1962. In a few short years, Vail became a world-renowned ski destination.

Also instrumental in the design and construction of nearby Beaver Creek and Arrowhead, Pete Seibert today is considered one of the great pioneers of ski resort development. The design and management of Vail and Beaver Creek have set the standard for resorts in both America and Europe. And all because a kid on skis in far away New England had a dream, and followed it to this own remote valley in the mountains of Colorado, Ski Country, USA

"SI TU VEUX VRAIMENT CONNAÎTRE
LA MONTAGNE LORSQUE TU SERAS
ARRIVÉ EN HAUT CONTINUE DE
GRIMPER."

3

A TOWN FROM SCRATCH, AND CURVES AHEAD

"We travel not to escape life, but for life not to escape us."
—Anonymous

At 7 a.m. the next morning Tom sat sipping coffee as he read about Vail's history on his cell phone. He knew Vail was not a former mining town, like Aspen or Breckenridge, where miners toiled in the 1800s hoping to strike it rich, but that Vail was created from scratch as a ski resort. He read that the main founder was a New England skier named Peter Seibert who was injured in Italy in World War II when a mortar exploded in a tree next to him and badly damaged his leg. Doctors told Pete he may never walk again, but he did walk and ski again. And in those post War years the American ski industry was growing rapidly with new ski resorts opening, so Pete left New England to find a mountain in the West where he could build his own resort. He first went to Aspen and became a member of the Aspen Ski Patrol and Aspen Ski School and then was manager of Loveland Pass (Colorado) Ski Area by the late 1950s, near what was to become Vail.

While at Loveland, Pete and a ski patroller there named Earl Eaton began looking where they could develop a new ski area, a dream they both had since meeting in 1947 in Aspen. Earl knew the local mountains well as a resident of the nearby town of Edwards who loved to roam in search of minerals with a Geiger counter in hand. Earl, then 35, decided to take Pete, then 32, to see an unnamed mountain that Earl had seen in summer and had thought it looked like a good skiing mountain with gentle rolling slopes and good snow conditions. In March 1957 they climbed to the top of that unnamed mountain that would later become Vail.

That morning they laced up leather ski boots and put climbing skins on their long 215-centimeter skis and tied long leather thongs around their ankles. With packs on their backs with lunches and other items for an all day trek, they climbed for seven hours until they reached the summit and looked back down on incredible skiing terrain: The north side they had climbed had gentle and steep slopes, and the south side had a series of open bowls where trees had long ago been burned off in wildfires, enabling future skiers to ski long distances without having to avoid trees. Pete was later quoted as saying they both instantly knew this was the place they were looking for. They also saw that the snow was a light, powdery quality and the wind was light in that area, both important factors for a ski resort. Earl had even placed snow-depth stakes on the mountain in summer so he could later gauge how much snow fell in that area.

After an hour at the top, the two men took what was probably the first downhill ski run at Vail mountain. The deep snow slowed them to a stop in some places, and they made the run down in less than two hours. Pete later said when he looked back up the mountain, he was already building the ski resort in his mind.

At that time the valley at the base of the mountain was home to sheep and cattle ranches, and the Greek sheepherders grazed their stock on the mountain in summer. Pete, Earl and two other founders began to buy up land in the Vail valley under the name of the Transmontane Rod and Gun Club. Their representative told the owner of the 520-acre Hanson Ranch, which sat right under Vail mountain, that four friends wanted to buy the ranch for hunting and fishing, a strategy aimed to not make it obvious that a ski resort was planned. But the owner, John Hanson, was not interested in selling for a year, until in 1958 the price of cattle fell and he decided to sell.

In 1959, Pete and Earl applied to the U.S. Forest Service for permission to build the ski resort. After getting their permit and buying the land, they next had to find 20 investors at $5,000 each. Investors were found in eight states, so the gun club was disbanded and Vail Corporation was formed in 1959. The project was then headed to build the ski runs, the chairlifts, lodging and the base town, and was done in time for opening in December 1962. A plaque sits today near the base of Gondola One in Vail Village telling the story and bearing the headline "This Is The Place. Pete Seibert's Dream."

• • • • • • •

Tom put down his cell phone and flipped through TV stations in his hotel room. He flipped to Channel 8 and watched Good Morning Vail, a local program of ski conditions, valley events and commercials, all promoting the good things of the area. There were commercials about the fur shops, jewelry shops, the clothing shops. Tom thought about the many sides of ski towns: the wealthy side with its luxury home-owners and their generosity through charitable organizations. He thought of the middle class workers living in condos and small homes, working in shops and other businesses; and he thought of the working poor, living in the smallest apartments or subsidized work housing and often living miles from the town but commuting to do the lowest paying service jobs.

At 8 a.m. Tom went downstairs to the lobby and met the Realtor he had called.

"Mr. Woods, nice to meet you. I am Bridget," she said. "You wish to look at homes and condos for sale and for winter rental, correct?"

"Yes."

"Your budget is up to $2 million? I can show you all kinds, including a rooftop penthouse rental in our West Vail Lionshead area with 5 bedrooms and access to a rooftop pool for up to $11,000 per night."

Tom laughed. "I won't be needing that one."

I'd like to see down the valley first, Tom said. So they drove west from Vail on Interstate 70, past the suburb of Eagle-Vail and saw a trailer park on right side, and at eight miles from Vail came to the town of Avon, where a massive Wal-Mart and Home Depot anchored a shopping area near homes, apartments, and an elementary school closeby at the foot of forested mountains.

"This is a regular town," Tom said. "I want to go in the Wal-Mart."

So they stopped and went in. The super-Walmart had 20 cashier bays. A manager walked by and Tom asked him: "Does this store do a big business?"

"Yes. In fact we are one of the top volume locations in the state."

As Tom and the Realtor drove west a few blocks they passed a massive Westin Hotel with a bronze statue of horses running in front of it, then the ski area Beaver Creek, then a luxury subdivision called Bachelor Gulch and a small ski area called Arrowhead, and a few minutes later, the town of Edwards with movie theaters, shops, restaurants, homes and schools.

"All these towns and more to the West are considered in the Vail Valley," the Realtor said. "In fact, our local TV station 8 has its station in Avon, not Vail."

Tom nodded his understanding.

"If you're looking for value, you can buy at Beaver Creek Ski Area and often get the same square footage for half the cost of being in Vail, and you've still got the world class Beaver Creek area there and a small town feel. But if you like Vail's European architecture and feel, it's an awesome place too. The grocery stores are in West Vail where there's a Safeway and a City Market. But no Wal-Mart."

"I'm getting the picture," Tom said. "It's the ski resort property syndrome."

"What type of residence to you have now?," she asked.

"I've got a little home in the hills above LA."

They looked at homes and condos in Avon. In Vail, she showed him condos. West of Vail a few miles, she showed him an old fashioned A-frame home at $1.5 million, a remodeled five bedroom home with hardwood floors and a floor-to-ceiling fireplace. The place had a ski lodge feel.

"I like this one," he said. "I'll think seriously about this one."

They parted at noon. "I'll be in touch with a decision shortly," he said.

Tom had a quick lunch and grabbed his ski gear and was ready to meet Eva at 1 p.m. at gondola one. He saw her walking up with her skis over her shoulder and he had a fleeting thought of Christine, who always insisted that someone else carry her skis so she would not wrinkle her ski coat or be uncomfortable.

"We meet again," Eva said. They boarded the gondola and she asked how his house hunting went.

"Very well. I got the Valley tour, down to Edwards. Where do you live?" Tom asked.

"I have a condo in Avon," she said.

"Do you live alone?"

"No. I have a roommate. A young lady."

Tom smiled and backed off his questions. "How about we ski the Northwoods run?," he said, looking at the ski run map.

"Sure," she said. "It's supposed to snow this afternoon, maybe heavy, let's get moving."

As they got off the gondola and clicked boots down into their bindings, big fat flakes started falling from low gray clouds. There was no wind, and Tom looked up into the silent gentle storm and opened his mouth to catch flakes.

"I love it when it snows like this. Not cold. Not a rough storm. Like a gentle rain. It's kind of romantic."

Eva looked at him and said nothing. Who is this guy?, she thought.

"Well, try to keep up if you can," she said. She skied off and slipped into Northwoods, an intermediate, with Tom on her heels. She went through bumps smoothly, her legs flexing like shock absorbers while her upper body was still. She swerved into trees and back out again when she found the snow too thin for safe skiing between the trees. When she slowed, he passed her and dropped into a deep chute of moguls. He thought for a moment that she was probably watching him, sizing up his skill, then he focused again on his turns, he slowed and turned on the tops of the moguls instead of the troughs. When he came to a stop, she slid to a stop beside him.

"You did not show off," she said. "Some guys would have blasted through the bumps as fast as they can."

"Are you calling me a sissy?"

"No"

"I've got nothing to prove, and knees to protect," he said.

She nodded agreement. "Follow me, I know a nice stash of fresh in some safe trees here. You like trees?"

"Sure, as long as they stay a few inches away from me."

Eva dropped down into a forested patch with trees evenly spaced and just enough snow to allow turns. She weaved left and right slowly, with Tom on her heels. The silent snow fell and a canopy of evergreen boughs was a few feet above them. They emerged back onto the open trail.

"That was lovely," Tom said.

"Lovely?" Eva said.

"What's wrong with that word?"

"Nothing. You just don't hear men say that much."

"I see. Well then, damn sister, that was a radical patch and we kicked ass. How was that?"

"No, that doesn't quite work for you either," she said.

Eva raised her ski pole and pointed to a yellow triangle-shaped sign in front of them that read "Danger: Curves and Hidden Obstacles Ahead."

"Are you up for it?" she asked.

"Lead on girl."

They skied through another patch of bumps and then patches of ice, thin snow and rocks jutting up from the snow.

They stopped and Tom was breathing hard. "Obstacles indeed," he said.

After another two runs the snow came down heavier and Eva said she had to leave and pick up her roommate.

"It's been nice to meet you," she said.

"Whoa," Tom said. "If I came in Pepi's tonight, maybe I'll see you."

"Maybe."

That night, Tom stood again in the doorway of Pepi's and asked for a table. He was seated and Eva walked by. She saw him and stopped and backed up to look at him.

"Well, hello there," she said. "The food bring you back?"

He smiled. He ate a nice dinner and asked Eva how late she worked. She said 11. He left and then showed up again at 10:30 in the bar for a drink. She walked by and stopped and looked at him.

"Are you stalking me?"

"That's such an unpleasant word," he said. "I was hoping to walk you home."

"Do I have to worry about you?" she said. "I don't really know you."

"What does your instinct tell you?"

"That's not always dependable."

"So I haven't asked you yet, but I'm guessing you don't have a boyfriend?"

"Nothing steady."

"Is there an unsteady?"

"There's a former friend who lives here who has become unsteady. Even a pest. I told him I had a new friend, a lawyer from Los Angeles."

"Oh, I'm not looking for trouble."

"I thought you were leaving in a few days."

"Yes. And I'd still like to walk you to your car."

When Eva got off work they walked though Vail Village toward a parking garage. As they walked by the Gore Creek, small groups of people walked by them. A group of four young men got up from sitting on the ground next to the bubbling river.

"Eva!," one of the men yelled. He stumbled over to her. She and Tom saw that he was drunk.

"Eva, I thought you might be getting off work now," he said.

Eva kept on walking. "That's my unsteady friend, Jason" she said to Tom.

"Wait," the man said and grabbed her arm. Tom pulled the man's arm away.

"Jason, leave me alone," Eva said.

"Who is your friend?," Jason said. They walked further and Jason and his friends surrounded her.

Tom spoke up. "Did you guys see that cop back there? He's huge."

Jason looked Tom over and said "There's no cop. Are you the guy from Los Angeles? She told me about you." Jason stumbled and slurred his words. "What do you do? Actor, lawyer, plastic surgeon? I could do some plastic surgery on you right now, maybe move your nose to the side, put it next to your ear. What do you say?"

"Maybe some other day," Tom said, and walked away with Eva beside him.

The guy jumped in front of Tom. "No, no, we're not done talking."

"I think we are."

"I think I'll put you on the ground now," Jason said.

"Not smart," Tom said. "You never know what kind of training someone has had."

"Oh really. Maybe your training was surfing or wait, I know...," Jason said as he picked up a ski pole from an outdoor rack next to a shop by the river. He raised the pole like a fencing foil and jabbed it at Tom. "Maybe you trained in fencing."

"Easy there," Tom said, backing away. Jason grabbed a second ski pole and threw it to Tom, who caught it. Jason jabbed close to Tom's head and Tom deflected the thrust.

"I could poke your eye out, LA boy." A few passersby stopped to watch as Jason threw more jabs.

"Well, we're lucky that new ski poles have blunt ends," Tom said. "In the old days, poles had a sharp metal point, but a lot of people still get hurt today with these spears."

"And you'll be the next one," Jason said. He jabbed at Tom's groin. Tom knocked it away and swung behind Jason, knocking his feet out from under him and he tumbled to the ground.

"Now I'm mad," Jason said.

"And drunk. What a shame," Tom said, as he reached in his pocket and positioned a small tube canister in his palm and put his finger on its button.

Jason lunged forward as Tom pulled the tiny tube of pepper spray from his pocket and sprayed it into Jason's face. Jason grabbed his eyes and screamed. As his friends leaned in to help, Eva pulled Tom away and they walked quickly away.

When they were out of sight from the group, she asked "What did you do?"

"A little pepper spray is a handy precaution to carry," he said.

"Have you done that before?"

"No, but it worked quite nicely, don't you think?"

Eva stared at him as they walked quickly. When they got to her car, she said "Why don't you come over to my place for a drink. I'll show you my condo. Here's my address."

"How nice," he said, and typed the address into his cell phone to use on the GPS directional app.

When Tom arrived a few minutes later and knocked on the door, she let him in and they went to the kitchen. She poured wine as Tom looked at photos on the wall and on the refrigerator door. A few vintage posters on the walls of the living room showed Vail in its early days.

He sat on the couch and Eva sat beside him.

"It's been quite a day," Tom said.

"That won't be the last we hear from Jason," she said.

"I'm not worried."

She leaned in to Tom close and kissed him.

"Very nice," he said.

"I've got something to show you," she said. She unbuttoned a few buttons on her blouse and lifted up a small sign, the size of a coffee coaster, hanging from the front of her bra. The tiny yellow triangle-shaped sign said "Danger: Curves and Hidden Obstacles Ahead."

Tom laughed aloud. "Yes, I can see the curves ahead," he said. "Where did you get that sign?"

"Ski shops carry them."

"Are you inviting me to see the curves ahead?," he said.

"No way, buster. I just wanted to make you laugh."

He kissed her and they talked for a few minutes and then he said "I think I should go. And you'll have to check on your daughter. I'm guessing she's sleeping soundly."

"How did you know I have a daughter? I didn't mention her yet."

"Photos on the refrigerator. And your comment about your young roommate."

"Do you like kids?," she asked.

"Love them. I probably still am one."

"Me too," she said.

He kissed her goodnight and said "I'll call you."

4

TRAIL NAMES AND GIRLFRIENDS
AND BACK TO LA

Words have meaning and names have power.
—Author Unknown

As skiers slide down ski runs, most of them are probably not aware of the meaning behind the names of the trails they are descending. For example, Vail's trail called Lost Boy is named for Martin Koether, who was 14 when he skied into Game Creek Bowl by mistake before it was developed and spent the night in a snow cave under a tree while rescuers searched for him. He made his way out of the bowl the next day. The trail Blue Ox refers to the folk legend of Paul Bunyan, a giant lumberjack of great strength whose companion was a Blue Ox named Babe. A trail called Gandy Dancer referred to the Gandy Manufacturing Company, which made tools used for laying railroad track, and the men who laid railroad track were nicknamed "Gandy Dancers". Vail's Ricky's Ridge is named for Ricky

Andenmatten, a Zermatt, Switzerland native who was one of Vail's first ski instructors.

Vail's Riva Ridge run is named for a ridge in the mountains of Italy where, in 1945 during World War II, the 10th Mountain Division achieved their best-known combat achievement. Vail's founder, Pete Seibert, was a member of that division that trained near Vail at Camp Hale. The trail Whippersnapper was cut as a child's adventure zone in 1987 and given the slang name for young rascals.

Vail's run called Whistle Pig, above Mid-Vail, is a nickname for the yellow-bellied marmot, a rock dwelling animal that whistles a warning when they perceive danger approaching. The trail Hairbag Alley refers to long-haired skiers that skied this gulch out of Northwoods in the 1970s.

The Vail back bowl called China Bowl is a long limestone formation that reminded early Vail skiers of the Great Wall of China. The Asian theme was continued as names were chosen such as when Vail opened Tea Cup, Siberia, and the Mongolia Bowls.

Other names of ski runs around the world have funny or double meanings. The Shaft & Climax run is at Mammoth ski resort. Psychopath and Devil's Crotch are two at Breckenridge. Kill the Banker and Big Woody are at Revelstoke. Big Doo Doo is at Alyeska. Steeper Than Hell, at Snowbird. Crested Butte is home to Sock It To Me, Body Bag Glades, Dead Bob's Chute and similar names. Kicking Horse area in Canada is home to CPR Ridge, Terminator Peak and Hail Mary. Oh My Jesus or OMJ is at Marble Mountain in Canada.

The next morning Tom was up early and walked into the village for breakfast. He walked past Gore Creek and saw the crystal clear water bubbling in the stream. He remembered reading about the issues over stream water in Vail and other ski areas. Ski areas take water from the creeks for snow-making, and run the water through high pressure machines to blow snow. The nearby towns also need water for citizens, and the U.S. Forest Service and the Bureau of Land Management have tried to keep water rights for themselves. Lawsuits have been the battle ground between the parties. Tom thought how even a simple stream is no longer simple as it runs where people live.

Tom had breakfast in a café and then boarded a chairlift to the top of the mountain's far east side. A brisk wind blew and he pulled his coat collar up around his neck. From the top he stopped and looked at the panorama of mountaintops around him. A few inches of fresh snow the night before sat like the whitest sugar, gleaming on the hills all around. He stood for a full minute looking at the snowy peaks, the puffy clouds and wide patches of blue sky above them. The alpine scenery and smells and snow under his skis created that fresh intoxicating feeling that a tourist gets when visiting a place so different from your own. For the first few days your senses are heightened as they take in all the stimuli and you revel in the new environment, such as the sights, sounds and smell of the ocean. Then after a few days, the feeling subsides, and you still enjoy the place, but not quite with the heightened feeling you had at first arrival. Tom was still reveling in first arrival sensations. He thought for a moment how much he liked to ski alone occasionally. He could stop whenever he wanted, take his own routes, not have to watch ahead or back to keep up with someone else, not even talk with others that caused a breaking of the silence of a pristine run from top to bottom. Of course, some people hate skiing alone, the loneliness of it, they crave the supportive comments of how good they ski, or the physical help to get up when they fall. For Tom, the conversations going up the chairlift were often enough.

He tightened his boots and looked at a ski run map. Then he slid down into a beginner run, called Tin Pants, to warm up. The snow was freshly groomed and packed. As he turned a little spray of snow kicked up from the edges of his skis. He looped left and right, feeling the slow curving turns. This was the way to start a day. He saw a patch of ungroomed powder next to thick trees on his left and he slid over to it and down the hill, making slow careful turns one to two feet from tree trunks in ankle deep powder, watching for hidden tree limbs under the snow that could trip him, but reveling in the feeling of shallow powder skiing.

When he got to the bottom, he rode the chairlift again and headed to the top for coffee at Two Elk Lodge. He remembered reading something years ago about this building burning down in an arson fire set by environmental activists angry at the ski area expanding into territory of the Lynx, an endangered cat. As he rode the chair up alone, he web searched the topic on his phone and found a Vail Daily newspaper story. He hit a button and an application on his phone began reading aloud the story. The story described that in 1998 fires burned down Two Elk Restaurant and several other buildings on Vail Mountain and caused $24 million in damage. In the early morning of Oct. 19, 1998, a man from Portland, Oregon ran along the ridge of Vail Mountain, lighting gas cans at Two Elk Lodge, Ski Patrol Headquarters and Chair 5, according to a memo filed by U.S. prosecutors. The man and others involved were allegedly part of a group called "The Family" that was associated with the Earth Liberation Front, an eco-sabotage group, the paper described. Two of the men then drove to Denver, where they sent an e-mail from a public library in which the ELF group claimed responsibility for the arsons "on behalf of the lynx," an endangered cat species living in the Vail area. The e-mail cited Vail's planned "Category III" expansion of ski terrain into lynx territory, which was named Blue Sky Basin on Vail's ski maps. The lodge was rebuilt, larger than the original. The Blue Sky Basin expansion continued as planned, opened in 2000 and has been a popular part of Vail Mountain.

· · · · · · ·

Tom did a couple more runs. In his fourth run, his phone rang so he stopped and clicked on the microphone dangling from his earbuds, and said hello. "This is Judge Harold Smith," the caller said. "I'm calling about the hearing next week for your client in the battery case on a police officer."

"Yes judge, thanks for calling."

"I have to be gone next week when that hearing is set, but I can hear your motion for dismissal tomorrow at 3 p.m. if you can be here."

Tom thought for a moment. It was vital to have this judge hear the motion, and to not delay for his client.

"Yes sir, I will be there. Thank you judge."

Tom hung up and slapped his ski pole on the ground in disgust. He had wanted to stay longer in Vail. Now he would have to book a flight for later today.

The next morning he woke up in his house in the LA hills and drove to the office. His dad greeted him and said "What are you doing back so soon?"

"I have a court date moved up to this afternoon."

"Are you still thinking of going back to Vail for the winter?"

"Yes, I'll talk with you more about it."

Tom worked his cases that morning and drove to the beach at lunchtime. The sun beat down on a beautiful December day. He pulled off his shoes and socks and rolled up his pant legs and walked on the sand. He dialed Eva's number.

She answered the phone with "Where are you, stranger?"

"I had to come back to LA for an emergency court hearing. I am walking on the beach right now, toes in the sand."

"Oh, was it something I said?"

"Not hardly," he said. "I'll be back soon."

"I hope so," she said.

As they talked, Tom felt drawn to her again, and he thought as he walked the beach that he should separate her from his decision to move to Vail as being a right move for him. It was a big step to leave his practice, his clients that depended on him. He drove back to meet his client at jail and then showed up in court early.

The judge called his case on a motion to dismiss. Tom stood next to his young client and Tom's thoughts flashed back to the day he was shot at in court. He glanced at this client, a much nicer kid this time, and he glanced at the court officer and the officer's holstered gun.

The judge called for the viewing of the police officer's body camera footage of the traffic stop. The young man got out of the car quietly as ordered by the officer, but then without warning flailed his arms wildly striking the officer, who slammed him to the ground and hand-cuffed him.

"What's the defense, Mr. Woods?" the judge said.

Tom stood and said "A neurologic condition with extreme muscle reaction caused by stress," he said. "Here's his doctor's statement, the medication he is on, and evidence of previous similar limb reaction under stress. It happened in his high school."

"Call your medical witness," the judge said.

Tom had the doctor explain. The prosecutor cross-examined. The judge raised his gavel.

"Seems an unusual but clear case to me," the judge said. "Dismissed."

Tom smiled and felt the best he had in weeks about a case. The young client and his family hugged Tom and left the courtroom.

Tom drove back to the office and his cell phone rang in the car. Christine's name showed on the caller ID.

"Hello, Christine."

"Your mother told me you were back in town."

"Yes. Have you been thinking about us?"

"Yes," she said curtly.

"Let's have dinner to discuss."

"What's the point?" she said.

"I was trying to be a gentleman."

"Well, you've failed on that score."

"Really. Where else have I failed?"

"You're shorter than I would prefer. Your taste in painters is too traditional. I mean, really, open your mind past Van Gogh."

"Ouch," he said.

"It's over Tom. I'm moving past you. Oh also, your upper class guilt is so obvious and pretentious. Just because you have money doesn't mean you have to go work in Africa or build houses for the poor. You can just give money to causes, you know, it's just as good. Why are you ashamed of being rich?"

"Who said I'm ashamed?"

"You act like money is a bad thing."

"So we should never get our hands dirty doing actual work with the poor, never actually talk to them?"

"What's the point? We do our part by giving money."

"I doubt that I could explain the point to you."

"Well don't even try," she said. "Good bye. Have a nice life."

Tom heard the line go dead, and he felt a relief. He drove back to his office and worked on case preparation for the day and then headed to his small home in the hills. He sat on his deck, looking over the city and called the Realtor in Vail. He arranged to rent a condo in Vail Village for the season and then started making a list of things he would take to Vail and things he would leave in his house in LA. He started making lists of his legal cases that he would have to assign to other lawyers. He set his planning notebook of lists down and looked out at the city as its lights began twinkling at sunset.

Pepi's Restaurant and Bar

5

A BUM MOVES TO VAIL

A person often meets his destiny on the road he took to avoid it.
—Jean de La Fontaine

The term "ski bum" has had many definitions but generally has meant a low-wage employee at a ski resort who is more interested in skiing than any job or career advancement. He or she lives to ski as much as possible. The typical ski bum, or surfing beach bum also, has been seen as a person of little education or ambition who may take two or three menial jobs and sometimes lives in dormitory buildings just to earn enough to be where skiing is. They often run the lifts, serve the food, clean the hotels and sometimes, in the view of others, seemingly avoid growing up and taking adult responsibilities.

But the type of bum in America has often changed with the economy. When the economy is good and the educated people can easily get high salaried jobs, fewer of these skiing Americans decide to move to ski resorts. The resort companies then must hire many low wage workers from abroad. But when the economy has slowed and many professionals are laid off their jobs, many of these engineers, lawyers, teachers and others decide to move where they can live a less stressful life, and they become the waiter with a doctorate degree who is quite happy waiting tables at night and skiing by day. Curious customers may ask and then remark to their friends "Oh yes, my waiter has a master's from Harvard in French literature," or "My server was an engineer at NASA."

And there are the wealthy bums, as some call them, the investment banker in New York who takes a winter off to ski at Jackson Hole, Wyoming; and there are the successful entrepreneurial bums, such as the web site designers or computer consultants or video game inventors who can live wherever they choose, so they carry their laptops on the mountain to stop and work a little in the ski lodge between runs. And of course, there are the rock stars or young retirees, who moved to the mountains or the beach after selling their company for tens of millions and are now seeing if they can get in 100 days of skiing this season. And so the ski bum has evolved and comes in many forms as they seek their own paradise.

Ski town locals sometimes are categorized by their timeline in the town. There's the "one and done bum" (one season) who is headed back to school or a job after his or her season of play. There's the "native" who grew up in the town and has never left. The "lifer" has been a bum in one or many places and has decades of stories he is glad to share. Sometimes the ski instructor and ski patroller is considered one of the bums, and sometimes they have been revered and admired as the professionals of the mountain.

• • • • • • •

It was an overcast and cool day in Los Angeles while Tom wondered what kind of bum he might now be considered. He loaded a small moving van and climbed into the cab of the truck in his driveway as his parents stood by.

"You're not taking much," Tom's father said. "You could have it sent, and you could still fly."

"I want to do the drive," Tom said.

Tom's mother said "Another adventure. Be careful."

Tom drove out of LA with his Range Rover in tow behind the moving van, and he headed northeast to Las Vegas. He planned to spend the night in Vegas, then the second night in Utah and then arrive in Vail the third night.

As the miles unwound he put on a jazz guitar and piano album by the Leonard Brothers. The happy jazz melodies made him feel good. He put down the window and let the breeze blow in his hair. He punched a button his phone and said "Call Eva." It dialed the number and her voice mail picked up.

Tom said "Hello, this is Franz," in his worst Austrian accent. "I am on the road in a Ryder van and will be in Vail on Wednesday night," he said. "I hope you to see you soon."

The hours flew by and about 6 p.m. he pulled into Vegas and drove to the back of a parking lot at Caesars Palace. He checked in to the hotel and had dinner, then looked around the Forum shops and played 21 and craps. A giddy young couple stopped near the craps table as friends congratulated them on getting married a few minutes earlier in the hotel. "I am so glad we got the Cleopatra Wedding Package," the bride said, still in her wedding dress. "Everything has gone perfectly."

Tom winced. He could not fathom getting married in Vegas. He wondered if he was too traditional. Open up your mind, he thought. Some people love this place. It would be a dream wedding and honeymoon for some people. Bring the whole gambling family and party until dawn. Tom liked Vegas, but for only about 24 hours, then he was always ready to move on. He had been there before for legal conventions, but the gambling and drinking scene was not his style. He went to his room early and was on the road the next morning at 6 a.m.

The drive through southern Utah fit his mood just right. The simple, stark landscape spurred him into a thinking mode, mulling over the issues in his life. He thought about the early Mormons coming into the state to find their new land and life. He thought about great skiing in the northern part of the state and how the Vail Resorts company had recently bought and linked two ski areas, Park City and Canyons, into the largest resort in the United States with 7,300 acres of skiable terrain. It was on his list to visit and ski. Tom stopped for the night in tiny Green River, Utah along I-70 and the next morning pushed on into Western Colorado flat desert country and toward Grand Junction. He passed long low red bluffs that reminded him of scenes in old western cavalry movies. He imagined long lines of Indians or soldiers riding under and on top of these bluffs. He pushed on past Glenwood Springs and went into Glenwood Canyon with its soaring red walls of rock next to the interstate and a winding river close to the highway. He remembered hearing that singer John Denver in the early 1970s had written part of his song "Rocky Mountain High" with a lyric that referred to people wanting to tear down the mountains to build more development, and that the singer was referring to a controversial plan at that time to widen the highway in Glenwood Canyon. But actually, Tom thought, the highway looked now like it turned out to not hurt the environment and was done with a clever design that allowed the eastbound and westbound lanes to be built stacked above each other in some places.

Tom arrived in Vail and drove to his condo in Vail Village. He met a condo building employee there and moved in a few pieces of his own furniture to augment the already furnished condo. Then his phone rang and answered a call from his brother, Pete, who was three years older and a hedge fund manager in Connecticut.

"What are you doing moving to Vail, you crazy bum?"

"Nice to hear from you, Pete. You've been talking to mom."

"She says you're going to ruin the family name. You'll be destitute and found frozen to a tree on some ski run."

"Yes, exactly, that is my plan."

"What is your plan? Do I need to come talk some sense into you, little brother?"

"Oh yes, please do try."

"I repeat. What is your plan?"

"I'm going to ski tomorrow until my legs hurt. I'm going to befriend the most lovely women I can find during Christmas. Then I may get a job as a snowcat driver or a deli sandwich maker."

"Oh I see. Anything to avoid be shot at in a courtroom, is that right?"

"Bite me," Tom said.

"Touchy, are we?"

"Only with hedge fund hedonists. Why don't you come visit me? You could even find new clients here."

"Probably true. I will call you soon. Take care of yourself."

Tom hung up and sat on a sofa in his new condo. A large window looked from the living room onto the ski runs. It was December 18 and a heavy snow storm settled over the valley that night. As Tom carried in his ski equipment to the condo he thought tomorrow would be a good day for fresh tracks. He walked around the condo and took in the look and feeling. He liked the heavy log furniture. The old fashioned stone fireplace. A painting of a skier in deep powder and another painting of a buffalo herd in a spring meadow hung on the wall. The place had a traditional feel and would be perfect for this season, he thought.

The next morning Tom woke early and turned on the Good Morning Vail TV show. A perky female host reported six inches of new powder had fallen on the mountain. Tom decided to head for the back bowls as soon as the lifts opened. He hurried out the door with his skis and caught the first gondola. As he settled in the gondola cabin, two snow boarders loaded in with him. One had a custom painted helmet with a tan colored image of a human brain on it, looking like a head of cauliflower. It looked gross to Tom, not funny as it probably was to the young boarder wearing it.

"That's a radical helmet," Tom said.

"Thanks, man," the boarder said. "I just got it yesterday. Ordered it online." He slapped it with his hand.

"Careful dude," Tom said. "Don't hurt your brain."

Tom remembered that he had read that helmet usage had increased from 25 percent of skiers and boarders in 2002 to 78 percent in 2015, according to the National Ski Areas Association.

The brainy boarder also carried a board with a V-shaped cut in the tail.

"What is that called?" Tom asked.

"That's the swallow tail board, named after the bird," the boarder said. "It's a powder board. It allows you to put your weight back on the tail and keep the nose of the board on top of the snow to stay higher when you're in powder."

Tom then looked at the other boarder, who carried a shiny new board with an image of a naked woman painted on it, with tiny coverings over her nipples and genital area.

"Now that is radical too," Tom said. "I've never seen that."

The young boarder said "It's my new Burton board from the vintage Playboy centerfold collection."

"Does it ever distract you, looking down at her while you're carving a turn?"

"Well, looking down at her can bring a man up," the boarder said smiling.

"Ah, yes," Tom said. "But do you get complaints that she's too revealing?"

"Oh yeah, man," the boarder said. "I rode a chair the other day with a mom and little kids and she ripped me a new one. She said I was corrupting her kids. I said lady, this is America, I'm free to carry any board I want, and you are free to look away."

Tom grabbed his cell phone and did a web search and found a news story with a quote from the chairman of Burton boards, who said he knows art can be offensive to some and inspiring to others. The story said that in 2008, about 150 people demonstrated near Burton's Vermont headquarters over the images of Playboy models and cartoons of self-mutilation on boards. Ten ski resorts in Vermont and the West also banned employees from using them on the slopes.

Tom asked the two young boarders: "Do you think skiers hate snowboarders?"

"Not most of them nowadays," one kid said. "But you know, a couple resorts still ban us. They want to be exclusive to skiers. They think we're dangerous, or that our wide boards plow the snow around too much and make icy patches. But we are slowly gaining respect. I'll bet without us the ski resorts would probably be losing money."

"There's old dudes boarding too, you just don't see them so much," the other boarder said.

Tom said "I agree you guys are probably getting a bad rap. But it reminds me of a joke I heard. How is a vacuum cleaner like a snowboard?"

"Don't know," the boarders said simultaneously.

"Both have a dirtbag attached."

"That's just cruel, man," one of the boarders said. "We've got skier jokes too. How are boarders and skiers different?"

"Don't know," Tom said.

"Boarders don't think they're better than everyone else on the hill."

"I see," Tom said.

"I got one," the other boarder said. "What creature needs two spears and an $800 jacket to keep upright on a hill?"

"A skier," Tom said. "I get the point."

"Boarders are creative too," one boarder said. "I saw a guy last year who had built a little fan engine on top of his board and when he got on flat terrain he flipped a button and the engine pushed that board along like a little boat cutting across the water. It was amazing."

Tom bid the youngsters farewell and headed to the back bowls. He slid into an open bowl and the powder came up to his ankles and then his knees in some spots. He began making turns and thought of advice he had heard on how to ski powder: The powder will slow you down, so keep up your speed. Float up and down. Do a floating turn as your weight comes up toward the surface. He was turning nicely, all alone in a field of untracked white, and he thought of Eva, he wondered what she was doing, his mind wandered, then he hit a crusty patch of snow and went down.

Tom put out his hands in front of him as he pitched forward and he went face forward into a crunchy patch of hard snow surface and then skidded into soft powder that coated his face in white makeup and slid down his neck and into his coat. "Oh, very suave," he said aloud to himself. He sat in the snow for a minute and slapped the ground with his pole. His skis were still on and he felt okay except for a stinging on his cheek where it had scraped across a hard piece of snow. Obviously I must focus in powder, he said.

He wobbled down to the chairlift and rode up by himself. He thought about concentration in skiing. There are times you can ski and turn with your body on automatic pilot while your mind thinks on other things, and there are times when you must focus.

When he got to the top of the lift he went in a lodge for a coffee and to check his injured cheek. His phone rang and he answered it.

"Hello, stranger," Eva said. "Where are you?"

"I'm in the Two Elk Lodge. I just had a flawless run down the bowl and I'm taking a short rest."

"Sound sweet. Are you a good powder skier?"

"Oh, I am the best," he said.

"I'll be the judge of that sometime soon," she said. "I've got a question for you."

"Yes?"

"Would you like to go a party tomorrow night? I have tickets to a special nightclub on top of Vail mountain. It's set up a few nights during the ski season to cater to upscale tourists."

"Sure. Let's meet for lunch and you can tell me more."

Tom skied a few more hours and met Eva at a small café. As they sat she held up a promotional card and read off it: "Decimo is an exclusive nightclub with a disc jockey, bikini dancers, laser lights, a pink dark glow light, electronic dance music, shots, women in glittering dresses and men in casual sweaters," she said. "Just steps away from the top of the gondola, which has heated seats and wifi, guests will enter a space that has undergone a carefully orchestrated transformation into the chic, dynamic nightspot that is Décimo."

She smiled. "I have tickets to the personal VIP bottle service. Our premium Champagne Table will have a premium view of the stage, six tickets, one bottle of Dom Perignon Luminous Magnum, two bottles of Ketel One Vodka, two 6-packs of Red Bull, two 6 packs of Aquafina, one 6 pack of Stella Artois, party favors and designated server."

"Wow, sounds like a rocking party," Tom said. "I have a casual sweater. Do you have a glittering dress?"

"I certainly do," she said. "And we've got six tickets, so I'll invite Summer and Autumn to bring their dates."

• • • • • • •

The next night when Tom and Eva rode the gondola to the top of the mountain, the sky was clear and stars shone through the crisp air. They entered the nightclub where the music was blaring and the laser lights flashing as bikini-clad dancers gyrated and people mingled while sipping cocktails.

"This is a different apres-ski," Tom said as they sat at a table for six.

Summer and Autumn came in, each wearing a glittering dress, and their dates wore sweaters.

"You ladies are lovely," Tom said.

One of the men said "I feel sort of 1970s in my sweater."

Tom talked a while and learned one of the men was a chef at a local fine restaurant and the other was a Realtor. For a half hour they conversed and danced as the cocktails flowed.

Tom was in mid-sentence when he felt a tap on his shoulder. He looked up and saw Jason looking down on him.

"Remember me?" Jason said.

"Of course."

Eva turned in her seat and her smile faded quickly. "Jason. Go away," she said.

Tom said "What a surprise to see you again. Are you sober this time?"

"Very sober. And you'll wish you had never met me."

"I'm already there," Tom said. "Let me ask you something, Jason. Have you heard the story of the rattlesnake and the rabbit?"

"What?"

"Sit for a moment and I'll tell you."

Jason pulled up a chair and listened as Tom talked.

"A rattlesnake was moving along the desert floor at sunset. He comes up behind a rabbit who is staring into the sun. The snake says 'Don't move. I am a rattlesnake. I'm going to eat you. It will all be over in a moment.' The rabbit says 'How do you know you can eat me? You don't even know me.' The snake says 'I am a deadly snake. You are a weak rabbit.' Then the rabbit turned around and faced the snake, and to the snake's horror he saw that the rabbit was actually a young tiger. The back of the tiger had only appeared to be a rabbit in the shifting light of the sunset. The tiger let out a roar and bit down on the snake's body, snapping off the head. The snake's head looked up at the tiger and said 'I should have been more careful.'"

Jason looked at Tom and said "So you think I am the foolish little snake and you are the big tiger?"

"Well, we don't know each other really, do we?" Tom said.

"Stay away from Eva," Jason said, "And I won't have to eat you, whatever you are."

Tom and Eva walked away and then talked and danced. Eva said "I'm sorry about him."

Tom said "You can always file a restraining order if he continues to harass you. Don't put up with it."

"Will you help me?"

"Of course."

They saw no more of Jason that night. As they rode the gondola down the mountain about midnight, Eva said "Look at the full moon. Wouldn't it be lovely to ski in the moonlight?"

"I've done that in Oregon," Jason said. "I have a friend who was an instructor at the Mt. Hood ski area near Portland. There's a ski run there that you can ski in the moonlight from Mt. Hood down to a nearby town called Government Camp. On clear nights, somebody would drop us off by car at the Mt. Hood parking lot and we skied on the trail for a half hour and then get picked up in the town. It was beautiful and the trail was pretty flat, so not many bumps to negotiate in the flat light. We would stop about halfway and have some wine and bread that we brought along. It was quite charming."

Eva said "I've got a friend who skied the base of the Matterhorn in Switzerland at night. There is a dinner offered, followed by a ski run down by moonlight, led by their ski patrol. I think we should go there."

Tom patted Eva on the knee and said "Maybe we will."

6

A BIG COMPANY

Wherever man goes to dwell his character goes with him.
—African Proverb

Tom awoke the next morning as the sun came in the bay windows of his condo that faced the ski runs. He looked on these mountains where the Ute Indians were believed to be the first residents. The valley offered good hunting for the Utes, who then avoided the harsh winters by moving West to the more arid desert-like land in lands of Western Colorado before coming back in the summers. The Utes nicknamed this Gore mountain range as "The Shining Mountains."

By the mid-1800s the first white settlers arrived in the valley. An Irishman named George Gore and the American explorer Jim Bridger were among the first white men in the area. They spent two summers hunting and exploring the peaks northeast of what is now known as Vail. A few years later, Bridger returned to the region and named the mountain range and valley after Gore.

By the 1870s, the Gore Range attracted fortune hunters as the news spread that its hills contained gold and silver. Mines were dug and railroad tracks laid to transport the metals. The miners drove the Ute Indians out of the area. One report said the Utes allegedly set fire to thousands of acres of trees in what is now Vail's back bowl skiing area, resulting in the deforested area that makes the bowls. Another report said a dry year caused natural fires that cleared off the back bowls.

When the minerals were gone, the miners left the valley. Sheep ranchers and others moved in. In 1939 construction began on Highway 6, running from Denver through the Gore Valley, and it later became Interstate 70. The original highway 6 project engineer was Charlie Vail, whose name was used for Vail Pass and later the Town of Vail.

Tom was making coffee when his phone rang and he answered.

"Son, I'm here to surprise you," the voice said.

"Dad, where are you?" Tom said.

"I'm at the Vail Valley Jet Center at the Eagle County Regional Airport. I brought the BJ. Can you come pick me up?"

"Of course."

A business jet, also called BJ for short, was daddy Scott Woods' favorite mode of transport. His law firm had a fractional ownership, often called a "time share", for half the cost of the jet, which entitled him to a certain number of hours of use when it was not being used by their other owner. Tom thought the jet was an unnecessary expense, but who could argue the convenience? He drove to the airport and picked up his dad and mom.

"This is a hopping little airport," his dad said. There are BJs and Lears and little Gulfstreams all over the place."

"The money is flying in for Christmas vacation," Tom said.

Tom's mother said "Tommy, I wish you would not refer to people as money."

Scott said "Son, there is such an emerging market for PJs, the personal jets. Cessna has its new Mustang, a six-seat twinjet that sells for about $2.5 million. I think we should look at that."

Tom nodded approval. "Why did you come so soon? I just saw you last week?"

"Well actually, our client Amos Moore invited us to his house in Beaver Creek to talk business for a couple days," Scott said. "We will stay there if you don't mind."

"Not at all, Dad."

Tom drove to the guarded gate at the entrance of Beaver Creek resort and was let through by the attendant. He drove to the Moore house driveway and looked up at the massive stone and wood home.

Tom's mother said "They just bought it and want to show it to us. Mountain modern architecture. Come in and look around."

"Some other time," Tom said. "I'll call you."

Tom drove back to his condo and then walked into the Village to have a relaxing breakfast and then explore the town. He sat in a small café and read the Wall Street Journal. Behind him he heard two servers talking about the Vail Resort company's employee housing that it has at its several Colorado resorts. The buildings are where more than 1,000 workers are housed for reduced rent to enable the low wage workers to live close to the slopes.

"I'm in the Breckenridge building," one server said. "Vail Resorts is offering us money to volunteer to take on an additional bed and roommate so they can get more employees in our buildings," one guy said as they debated whether to take the offer.

"It's more money," the other server said. "I'm sure glad they give us a free season ski pass."

Tom was curious and so looked up Vail Resorts on his phone. He read that Vail Resorts Inc. is the largest ski resort company in the world. It owns resorts in Colorado, Canada, Australia, Utah, Minnesota and other locations, and was buying more as it expands. It also owns luxury resort hotels, sports shops and real estate companies that sell or develop homes at the base of ski resorts. Tom read that in recent months Vail Resorts had bought Canada's huge Whistler-Blackcomb Resort for $1.06 billion and then made its first East Coast purchase by getting Vermont's Stowe Mountain Resort for $50 million. That sent Vail Resorts' stock price up to more than $180. He read that the previous season the company sold more than 650,000 Epic season ski passes at $809 apiece, totaling $525 million in cash, and that there are Epic Pass holders in all 50 U.S. states and in 99 countries. He read that when the pass skier loads on a chairlift, a scanner picks up data from the pass, enabling the company to track the skier's location and later send a targeted marketing email to the passholder.

Vail Resorts is not headquartered in Vail, but in the north Denver suburb of Broomfield, in a 10 story glass office tower. It reportedly employs 30,000 people. In 1980 Vail Resorts opened the Beaver Creek ski resort 13 miles west of Vail as another premier ski resort that is especially child friendly with many beginner runs. Like Vail, "the beav" resort developed with numerous lodges and stores at its base and a short drive downhill in the town of Avon. And then through Vail Resorts Development Company (VRDC), the company developed Bachelor's Gulch, on the west side of Beaver Creek, one of the most upscale resorts with more than 100 slopeside luxury homes and its own small ski area by the same name. And adjacent to that area Vail Resorts bought another small private ski area, called Arrowhead, which enabled Vail Resorts to link Beaver Creek with the two smaller resorts to the west, allowing skiers to crisscross between the three. Beaver Creek was known as the Colorado home base of former President Gerald Ford, who had a house in the Strawberry Park section of Beaver Creek. Tom read that the company tried to be good neighbors with the towns it operated properties in, and that one way was having a pledge to put zero waste to landfills by 2030 and zero net emissions by 2030, and by helping fund affordable housing projects in its areas.

Tom ate his breakfast and went for a walk through Vail Village. He stopped in an art gallery and looked over the bronze sculptures and oil paintings. A gallery employee walked up to him.

"What kind of art do you like?" she said.

"Oils mostly," Tom said. "I paint a little myself."

Tom stood before a large painting of two skiers coming down a slope. Their clothes were in bright reds and blues, with a white spray coming up from their boots and a pink sunset behind them.

"We also specialize in western art and contemporary," the lady said. "Do you like contemporary?"

"Yes, but I've been told I need to open my mind past Van Gogh," Tom said.

"There are a lot of styles to appreciate," the woman employee said.

Tom looked around and asked how business was for the gallery and for lodging in Vail before Christmas.

"It's all picking up steam," the lady said. "When we have lots of snow, the lodging marketers publicize it worldwide and bookings go up and the stores benefit. They say that international guests are 25 percent of our business."

"Where are they from, mostly?" Tom asked.

"Mexico City, Brazil, Europe, Australia," she said.

"Very international," Tom said.

• • • • • • •

At 11 a.m. Tom suited up and went up the hill for a few runs. He then went to the Mid Vail lodge for lunch and found himself sitting next to a group of Australians, listening to their conversation.

"That last run was a real ripper," one of the middle aged men in the group said.

"Yeah, nothing like that in Melbourne," another said.

Tom leaned over and said "Excuse me. May I ask if you all are from Australia?"

"Good guess," a young woman in the group said. "Was it our accents?"

Tom nodded yes and said "I'm rooting for more of you to come ski in America."

The group burst into extended laughter at Tom's comment.

"Young man," said an older man to Tom, "the word 'Root' in Australia means sexual intercourse. It does not mean to encourage something, like in American slang. We'd think you're a real bogan if you said that again."

"What's a bogan?" Tom said.

"It's a redneck, an uncultured person," a young girl in the group said. "I doubt that's you. What kind of work do you do?"

Tom decided to slant the truth of his occupation. "I'm an electrician."

"Oh, a sparky!" said the girl.

"Are you serious?" Tom said.

"Yes, that's our word for electrician," she said.

"You Aussies are delightful," Tom said. "Are there many of you that come to Vail?"

The oldest man in the group explained that about a million Australians travel to American ski resorts annually, and that Vail Resorts had recently bought Australia's Perisher Ski Resort, the largest ski area in the Southern Hemisphere.

"It's on the southern edge of the island and has a ski season of June to October," the old gentleman said. "There are not many U.S. skiers going to Australia to ski, but there are many Australians going to the U.S. As a Vail season pass holder, we can ski all year around on one pass. "

Tom knew about year-round ski travelers, but had never met one.

The group and Tom finished their lunches and Tom followed them outside. They met an instructor and headed down the hill in a group lesson. Tom followed them from a distance and listened to the chatter among the group, which was comprised of mostly intermediate skiers.

"This run is another ripper!" one of the men said as they came to a stop.

The instructor counted to make sure all students were in place and then told them he wanted them to work on parallel foot placement.

"On this run, follow me and work on keeping your feet closer together, but still slightly separated, and push harder on your outside ski to make it turn on its edge and carve that turn," he said.

They went down the hill in a smooth group going single file, and Tom followed again at a distance. The instructor and the students were laughing and having a good time. Suddenly Tom thought that instructing was something he might want to do.

He skied on to the bottom and caught a chair up with a man in a blue coat and a child seated beside him. When Tom looked at the man he realized it was another instructor.

"What does it take to become an instructor?" Tom asked.

"Well, you can be certified or non-certified," he said. "And if you certify, you can be level 1, which is only for teaching beginners, or level two which is for teaching intermediates, and finally level three, which is expert level. You can teach children or adults or both. You can do part time or full time. I would do some research on the Web and then talk to our ski school."

"Is Vail hiring?" Tom said.

"All the time," the man said.

"Do you like it?"

"I love it. It's part time for me. It pays very little, but it's the time on the hill and with people that is the best."

Tom went home that night and met Eva for dinner. He asked what she thought of him becoming an instructor.

"Oh no you don't buster," she said. "You don't need to give lessons to flirty young women from around the world."

Tom smiled. "Okay, I'll teach only old men and children."

"That would be acceptable," she said.

They talked for a few minutes and then Eva said, "Tomorrow, let's get away from here and go ski Arapahoe Basin. It is just a short drive east of here and our Vail season passes are good there."

Arapahoe Basin ski area

7

JEALOUSY, THY NAME IS DANGER

Jealousy lives upon doubts. It becomes madness or ceases
entirely as soon as we pass from doubt to certainty.
—Francois de La Rochefoucauld

Arapahoe Basin is a smaller ski area compared to Vail, and has some of the highest skiable terrain in North America. Half of the ski area is above timberline and has open bowl skiing sometimes into early July because of the slower snow melt there. It opened in 1946 with the ticket price for one day of $1.25.

Tom and Eva got up early the next morning and drove the 40 minutes east from Vail to Arapahoe. They drove past the town of Dillon, which lays in a valley, and they drove the winding two-lane highway past the Keystone ski area and then higher until they reached the A-basin parking lot.

"It is amazing how much skiing is in this area," Tom said.

"I know. I was wondering, when did you learn to ski?" Eva said.

"I was about five years old. My dad took me to Big Bear and Mammoth. I loved skiing immediately. Even more than I loved surfing."

"I've never surfed," Eva said.

"Maybe we can go sometime together. It's definitely involves less clothing and equipment."

As Tom and Eva rode up a chairlift a pair of snowboarders sat beside them talking, so Tom asked a question.

"Is boarding similar to skateboarding?"

"Definitely," one boarder said. "Turns, balance, lots of it."

"You ever tried it?"

"Not yet," Tom said.

"You might like it. Some people do both, ski and board."

"I like that idea," Tom said.

"Would you be goofy or regular?," the young boarder said.

"Pardon me?"

Eva laughed and said "Even I know what that is. If you stand on the board with your right foot near the nose of the board, it's called a goofy stance. If your left foot is nearest the nose, you are regular."

"How do you know what you should be?" Tom asked.

The young boarder said "If you balance on your left foot while kicking a ball, then you should should have your left foot forward on the board, and you are a regular."

Tom thought and said "Yep, I'm a regular."

"And from there," the boarder said, "it's about the motions in the head, and shoulders and hips and feet as you make your turns and get an edge on the board. It's a flowing. It's like your whole body is connected and moving in a wave sometimes."

Tom and Eva got off the chair and watched the boarders sail away. They skied about 10 runs before the day turned colder and they decided to return to their car at 2 p.m. As they pulled around the parking lot to head back down the mountain and toward Vail, Eva said "Oh no."

"What's wrong?"

"Circle around again," she said.

Tom drove around the lot again.

"I see Jason's red pickup truck following behind us. I see him in it."

"Call the police," Tom said.

Tom drove another circle around the lot and thought he had lost the follower, so he drove back onto the highway and headed down the mountain.

Eva screamed. "He's behind us and is aiming a gun out the window."

Tom heard a loud pop and then another.

"Put your head down," Tom said as his pressed the accelerator hard. His car sped ahead and swerved around a turn.

Jason's truck closed the distance and slammed into the back of Tom's car.

Tom sped up again and opened distance between the two vehicles.

"Is he crazy enough to try to kill us?" Tom asked. "Or just scare us."

"I don't know."

The red pickup closed the gap again and both vehicles' tires screeched as they carved into a right turn, with a rocky slope on the right side and a forest of green trees on their left.

The road straightened for a short space and the pickup hit the back of Tom's car again.

"Tom!" screamed Eva.

Tom struggled to keep the car steady and looked in the rearview mirror as the pickup gained speed, wildly lurched and then pulled up alongside Tom's car on its driver's side.

Tom and Eva looked at Jason who was waving a silver handled pistol. As they looked at him, a loud horn began honking in front of them and they looked up to see a car coming head on at them in Jason's lane from around a bend.

Jason spun his steering wheel to avoid the oncoming car and the pickup truck careened off the road and into the forest.

Tom braked his car hard and slid to a stop on the shoulder of the road.

"Are you okay?," he said to Eva.

"I think so."

The oncoming car skidded to a stop and pulled onto the shoulder. Tom and Eva got out and ran to the spot where Jason's truck had flown off the road and into the trees. Tom could see broken branches where the truck had gone down a short hill, bashing off the side of trees. He and Eva scrambled down the hill, between the trees, and quickly came to a clearing where a stream ran along the valley floor. The truck was wedged between two trees, its windshield broken as if a body had flown through it. They went a few yards more and found Jason's body lying at the edge of the stream, face down as water ran over his body.

Tom crouched and looked at Jason and then rolled his body over. Jason moaned and Tom saw a ghastly sight. A huge gash extended from Jason's mid-chest to his lower abdomen. Organs protruded and blood gushed into the stream. Eva walked up to the scene and gasped when she saw it.

"I'm...cold," Jason moaned.

"You went through the windshield," Tom said.

"I'm....sorry," he said. "I'm not a bad person. I just wanted to scare you away from her."

Tom and Eva stared as the clear water filled quickly into a red swirling pool around Jason's body.

"Help me up," Jason said.

"You can't," Tom said.

Jason looked down at his abdomen and screamed. "Oh God. Help."

"I don't think there's time," Tom said.

Jason held out his hand to Tom, pleading with his eyes for a human touch.

Tom hesitated and then slipped his hand into Jason's.

"I'm sorry," Jason said again. The young man shuddered for a few moments and then closed his eyes and his hand and body went limp, and his eyes closed.

"He's gone," Tom said, looking back over his shoulder to Eva.

8

MEET THE PARENTS

A person with a new idea is a crank until the idea succeeds.
—Mark Twain

In the days following the accident, Tom and Eva talked with the local police and sheriff's department about Jason's threats and the accident. With the eyewitness description from the third driver, who had almost crashed into them, investigators cleared them of any fault in the accident. Tom and Eva went into the Christmas week with a thankfulness to be alive.

Tom decided to try being a ski instructor. He went through the review process with Vail Resorts and was hired as an uncertified part-time instructor to start out teaching beginners. He told his supervisors he planned to take the tests to be a certified higher level instructor.

Each night Tom and Eva walked the streets of Vail that were decorated with Christmas lights and garlands and paper lanterns. They ice skated with Sophie and other children at an ice rink in Vail Village and joined carolers singing in the street. It was a relaxing time for them amid the bustle of the holiday.

Tom's parents were still in town and he told them about his relationship with Eva. His mother was quiet on the subject, and his father said he was sure Eva was a nice girl. Tom gathered his parents and Eva and Sophie for dinner at his condo on Christmas Eve. When his parents arrived, Sophie greeted them first at the door.

"Hello Mr. and Mrs. Woods," she said.

"Well, you must be Sophie!" Tom's mother said. "You are a delight."

Tom introduced everyone and gave his parents a tour of the condo and he then settled into carving the turkey.

"Tom this is a lovely meal," his mother said as they all stood in the kitchen and drank wine and looked at the food Eva was fixing.

As they sat a light snow fell and Tom put classical music on a low volume by the dinner table. The bay windows by his kitchen and living room showed the light fading behind the ski runs.

When they were all seated and began eating, Tom's father asked Eva where she was from.

"Virginia," she said.

"Oh, I love Virginia," he said. "Lovely country. And many horse ranches."

"Dear...," said Tom's mother to Eva, "Are you from horse people?"

"Pardon?" Eva said.

Tom said "You know, horse people. A creature with the back part of a horse and the front part of a person."

"No," Eva said. "We had no ranch or horses."

"What did your people do, dear? Were they successful?" Iris Woods said.

"Mother, really," Tom said.

Eva smiled and showed no irritation at all.

"Oh yes. My father managed a hardware store that was very successful."

"Oh, how nice," Iris said. "And are you divorced?"

"Yes."

"What work does your ex-husband do?"

"Mother, you're being nosy again," Tom said.

Eva began to answer when Sophie jumped in and said "My father is a Congressman."

Tom stopped and looked up from his plate. "Eva. You said he was a banker."

Eva nodded. "Yes, he was a banker before he ran for Congress."

Scott Woods said "Is he a Republican or Democrat?"

Sophie said "Independent. And so am I."

"Yes you are," Eva said. And they all laughed.

"Well," Scott said. "We will have to talk politics sometime, Sophie."

After dinner, Iris approached Eva alone in the kitchen and said "Dear, what happened to your marriage?"

Eva hesitated and looked at Iris. "Let's say that he found marriage too constricting."

"I understand dear," Iris said. "Men can be such animals. But not my son. He is the best of the litter."

"I'm so glad to hear that," Eva said.

"But," Iris said, "this is a new idea for our family for someone to become a ski bum. We are a bit worried for Tom. His destiny has been set, until now."

"Well, maybe he will make a new destiny."

On Christmas morning Tom went to Eva's condo and watched Sophie opening presents. The days that week passed quietly for them. Tom's parents went back to Los Angeles and Tom took the time to walk the area of his neighborhood and meet his neighbors.

On New Year's Eve, Tom and Eva and Sophie watched Vail's Annual Torchlight Parade on the mountain, where ski instructors and Vail locals ski down a run in single file line in the dark as they hold glowing sticks.

"That's magical," Tom said as the sight filled his eyes and the torches seems to dance left and right by themselves above the pale glow they made underneath on the snow.

"It's fun to be in that line too," Eva said. "I've done it once. The lights sparkle ahead of you."

As the glowing line came to an end at the bottom of the run, a fireworks display followed.

Sophie stood on the wooden deck railing of Tom's condo and Tom steadied her as she got a better view of the fireworks.

On New Year's Day, Tom and Eva decided to ski the morning despite the crowds that kept many locals off the mountain. They used a special application on their phones to check the lift line wait times and they skied among the lifts with the shortest lines.

As they rode up a lift Tom said "You know there's a tiny radio-frequency computer chip in our season passes and even in lift tickets that records where we go on the mountain and how many vertical feet we ski."

"I know," Eva said. "I don't care that I'm tracked, but some people object to it. I read that a Colorado ski instructor started producing and selling an aluminum shield that blocks the radio signals. Makes you wonder where the ski industry will be in 50 years."

"Here's what I see in the future," Tom said. "No more long walks for visitors from parking lots or garages to the chairlifts while hauling our equipment. I see us arriving in our solar-powered cars that are driven totally by computer. A robot meets you at your car and carries all your equipment to the base lodge as you walk beside him, or you may even ride in a sidecar attached to him. You tell the robot what you want for lunch and he communicates that to the restaurant on the mountain, which will have your order ready when you get there. And maybe at the end of the day you push a button on your cell phone and your auto-drive car comes to meet you at the base lodge where the robot loads your equipment into your car for you."

"Well," Eva said. "I suppose the ski instructors and patrollers and lift operators could all be robots too."

"That would be no fun at all," Tom said.

"Do you know that we already have private clubs with valet service? At Beaver Creek, there's one called the White Carpet Club. Visitors driving with their gear are greeted by staffers in the parking garage, ready to help unload. Or if the gear is rented, then the staff has it ready before visitors arrive. The staffers also help with dinner reservations and getting kids suited up at the base at the club location close to a ski lift."

"It sounds like the future is almost here," Tom said.

"What else do you see in the ski future?" she said.

"You'll laugh," he said.

"Try me."

"Well, when I'm too old and bent to ski anymore, say when I am 100, I envision myself putting on virtual reality goggles and stepping into a fantasy world ski resort that will seem totally real. While I'm sitting on my couch, I'll move my arms and legs and I'll be skiing on the most brilliant blue day or in the wildest snowstorm, even jumping off ledges that I never could do in real life or skiing in powder up to my neck and never falling, or at least never getting hurt. The technology could get us there for all kinds of sports like that."

"You're a dreamer," she said. "Hey, I've got an idea. Let's go ski Aspen tomorrow."

"Won't it be crowded?"

"Let's go anyway."

Schneehuhnjäger auf der Hochebene Norwegens.
Nach der Natur aufgenommen von Vincent Verde in Düsseldorf.

9

VISITING ASPEN AND CHAIRLIFT RAPELLING

How glorious a greeting the sun gives to mountains.

—John Muir

When did skiing on snow first develop? Cave paintings on rocks in Europe clearly show people on skis and have been dated to 5,000 years ago. Perhaps even much earlier, some man or woman probably looked down at their feet in the snow and realized that they might not sink so deep if they stood on a piece of wood and shuffled forward. And perhaps their second thought was to use a strap to keep their foot on the crude ski or snowshoe and so was born a new way to travel. Soon hunters on snow were following their prey across Russia, Asia and the artic wearing skis. By the 1700s, members of the Swedish army trained on skis and the Norwegian army reportedly held contests in the 1760s involving skiing down slopes and around trees. Skiers first used one long wood pole for balancing, braking and turning. Skiers began to use two ski poles in 1741, giving more balance than one pole could provide.

In 1868 some European summer mountain resorts became commercially viable for winter sports when city-dwellers could reach them in winter by train. The sport grew and by the 1880s began to shift from Nordic skiing (Norway cross-country skiing on flat land) to the new and exciting Alpine skiing (downhill skiing in the Alps mountains).

In 1914 in the United States, the first ski operation opened at Howelsen Hill in Steamboat Springs, Colorado with ski jumping featured; and was followed in 1923 by a small downhill ski operation at Eaglebrook School in Deerfield, Massachusetts where a rope tow was later used.

In 1924 the first Winter Olympics was held in Chamonix, France with cross country ski events only, but gained attention for the sport. In 1934 the first rope tow to pull skiers up a hill was installed in the U.S. in Woodstock, Vermont and included a continuous loop of rope running over several wheels and was driven by the rear wheel of a Model A Ford. The success of the 1932 Winter Olympics in Lake Placid, New York, drove an interest in winter sports and especially downhill skiing. Businessmen began to see the potential of the sport and in 1936 the first winter destination resort in the U.S. was developed at Ketchum, Idaho by W. Averell Harriman, the chairman of the Union Pacific Railroad, as a way to increase ridership on his passenger trains in the West. Harriman was a skier who believed America would support ski resorts like those in the Swiss Alps, so he hired an Austrian Count to travel across the western U.S. to locate an ideal site for a winter resort. After seeing many sites, the Count decided the former mining town of Ketchum was ideal, so Harriman quickly built the Sun Valley Resort and it opened to international publicity. Movie stars including Clark Gable, Gary Cooper and Ingrid Bergman came to ski at the new resort.

Also in 1936, efforts began to develop the former mining town of Aspen, Colorado into a ski resort, although it would be 10 years later when the first chairlift, lodges and ski races opened in the town. The sport kept growing and the metal ski was invented early in the

1950s, replacing wood. In the 1960s came the plastic boot to replace the leather boot. More resorts opened across the world as attention grew for the new sport, driven by publicity from ski racing, celebrities and media outlets covering growing numbers of middle class people wanting to enjoy winter sports.

. . . .

After Tom and Eva planned their trip to Aspen, the next morning broke bright and crisp with a light new snow from overnight in the valley. Tom and Eva left at 7 a.m. and drove two hours to Aspen with a plan to ski in the morning and then shop in the afternoon.

They met in the morning with an on-mountain ski ambassador who led them to a few of the secret ski run shrines of Aspen, which are about 100 memorials across Aspen's four ski mountains that consist of photos and memorabilia attached to trees. Most are hidden in the trees and were secretly built by varied people. Some honor celebrities such as Elvis Presley and Jerry Garcia. There's a 9-11 shrine, several for dogs, sports, sports stadiums and teams.

Tom and Eva skied up to a shrine for author Hunter S. Thompson. The site contained pictures, posters and a pot honoring the late Aspen area resident.

"This is neat that people do this," Eva said.

"Sometimes the ski patrollers remove shrines, but new ones spring up," the ambassador said.

Tom and Eva skied for two hours and then loaded on the Tiehack Express four-passenger lift about 11 a.m. and were mid-way up the mountain when the lift stopped.

"I don't like it when they stop," Eva said, as she pulled the safety bar down to prevent sliding off the chair.

They talked for a few minutes and a cold wind blew then as they continued to sit. Tom pulled the collar of his coat up around his neck.

He looked down at the ground again and said "Not too much of a drop if we have to rapel."

"Ha. You are so funny," she said.

The two of them sat alone on the lift for 15 more minutes. The temperature was in the 20s.

"I'm getting cold," Eva said. "You know, there are times when they have to evacuate people off chairs."

"I've only heard of it," Tom said.

"Me too."

A few more minutes passed and a ski instructor came by and tried to throw hand warmers up to stranded passengers. Another person came by and said it could be a long wait, that it could be an electrical problem.

"That sounds bad," Tom said. "I don't like to wait."

They kept their fingers and toes moving to stay as warm and as limber as possible. Tom tried to call the ski patrol on his cell for information about the situation, but did not get through. Another 15 minutes passed, which seemed like an hour to the shivering couple.

"Eva," Tom said. "I'll tell you a secret about me. I really don't like to wait. Anywhere."

"So?"

"What if I told you we could get down by ourselves?"

"How in the world...." she said.

"I carry a small nylon rope in my pack. It has enough knots that we can lower ourselves down safely. Then I would pull the rope down and we ski away. Theoretically, it's as simple as that."

"Theoretically," she said.

She looked at Tom. She looked at the ground and judged it not too far.

"We're not supposed to do that. We could lose our ski passes."

"Our one day pass, yes," he said. "Versus sit here for another hour."

He frowned at her.

She frowned at him.

"Did I mention I hate to wait?" he said.

"Well, I am not scared of heights," she said. "I used to mountain climb with ropes when I was a teenager. But we could fall."

"Yes we could. Or we could be here for hours and get frostbite."

Eva said nothing. She was thinking.

"Can you take a calculated risk?" Tom said.

"I'm dating you, aren't I?"

"Do you trust me?"

She smiled a sweet smile at him and nodded yes.

"And is your arm strength strong?" he asked.

"Buster, I could crush you like a bag of popcorn," she said.

Tom pulled off a thin fanny pack he carried. He unrolled a long yellow nylon rope, thin, but very strong.

"We'll go slow and steady, one knot at a time. I'll go first," he said.

"You bet your ass you will," she said.

Tom looped the rope around a bar in the center of the chair and dropped the end toward the ground. It hit the ground with a few feet to spare. He pulled on the rope, testing it for stability, and then he slid off the chairlift and put all his weight on the rope. Eva was a little surprised that Tom showed no hesitation at all.

Somebody in a chair behind them yelled "Hey look at that guy!"

Tom lowered himself down the rope, hand over hand, skis dangling from his feet, and he was down in less than a minute, standing solidly on the ground.

Eva looked down at Tom, and then gave him a finger gesture of contempt.

"I don't mind that," he said. "As long as you come down here right now."

She grabbed the knots and lowered herself off the chair. She felt strong. She lowered herself hand over hand. The knots seemed small but provided good support. She was down in 30 seconds. Tom pulled the rope down and tucked it in his coat pocket and they skied away quickly as people in other chairs yelled "Hey, what about us?"

Media stories reported later about 80 skiers and snowboarders were evacuated that Wednesday from the malfunctioning chairlift. Ski patrollers had removed the passengers from the lift after noon and the evacuations took about two hours with passengers being belayed down. Aspen Skiing Co. said in a statement that the lift had a faulty emergency circuit relay. Company officials made the decision to evacuate the lift about an hour and 10 minutes after it had stopped.

The Aspen Times reported that a woman who was stranded on the lift called The Aspen Times at 12:30 p.m. to complain that she wasn't getting enough information from ski patrol when she had called on her cell phone, and she wondered what the policy was on how long to wait to begin evacuation. An official said in the story that there was no set amount of waiting time that triggers an evacuation because most times mechanical repairs get the lift moving again, and weather temperatures play a role in whether evacuations have to be started sooner.

Evacuations were done by patrollers using a canvas seat that was attached to a rope held by another patroller on the ground, and ropes were put beneath each passenger's arms and a shoulder. The people were then lowered down. An Aspen Times reporter who watched the teams lower people said most passengers were calm but that one man was irate and screaming that he would be late to pick up his child from ski school.

Tom and Eva skied down to the base lodge and went in to get warm.

"We seem to have escaped," Tom said as they sat having a beer at a bar.

"Admit it," Eva said. "You loved that. You've been waiting years, carrying that rope, just to have that adventure today."

"No, I will not admit it," Tom said.

As they ate lunch at the lodge, Eva told Tom about Vail's own lift accident history.

A 1976 gondola accident at the Lionshead area of Vail Mountain killed four people and was the worst ski lift accident in Colorado history. Two gondola cars, each carrying six skiers, fell to the ground on March 26, 1976. Three people died instantly and a fourth man died later. Eight other skiers were injured. A Forest Service report described the problem as a fraying "track cable," which guides the wheeled gondola cars past lift towers, the Denver Post reported.

She described other accidents across the ski industry. In 1978, four people were killed and 31 injured at Squaw Valley when a cable car detached in a storm. In 1985, a bullwheel at Keystone resort failed, sending waves down the line that threw 60 people off the Teller Lift, two of whom later died from their injuries. That accident was blamed on a manufacturing defect and resulted in many lawsuits targeting the lift maker. In 1995, four chairs plunged from Whistler's Quicksilver lift, killing two and injuring four in an accident that traced back to design flaws in the lift's braking system, the Post reported.

Tom sat back after hearing Eva describe the accidents.

"How do you know all that?"

"I just have a good memory for what I read."

"Are you sure you're not a personal injury lawyer?"

"Very sure," she said.

As they walked around the shops of Aspen that afternoon, they stopped in the clothing stores and art galleries. In one gallery they saw a huge black and white photograph of a lion squinting into the wind as its mane blew back in the breeze. Regal. A golden frame around the photo emphasized the lion's royalty.

Eva motioned to the gallery employee and asked how much the price was on the photograph.

"It just sold for $125,000, madam," he said.

"Really?"

"Really."

"I must practice my photography," she said.

They then walked a few blocks to the Aspen Art Museum, a four story building that houses contemporary art. They saw a display of pillows stacked on a cabinet and read that the artist intended them to be seen as building blocks in a geometric pattern. Another display had cigarette butts arranged artfully in an ashtray. Another had framed white pieces of paper torn in different angles. Tom and Eva looked quizzically at each other as they passed each display.

They went to an outdoor rooftop display atop the building. Several cement blocks lay on the rooftop in a display.

"Is that a cement log?," Tom asked.

"Perhaps it represents a tree laying in the forest," Eva said.

"I don't understand contemporary art."

"Or maybe we just don't appreciate it," Eva said. "Look at these reviews on the Web of these displays. Brutal."

After 30 minutes they left the gallery and walked to a café for coffee. Ski videos played on a monitor in a corner.

"Let's change the topic from art to film," Eva said. "Did you ever see the movie Aspen Extreme? Nice little film about two young guys who move to Aspen and get jobs and live the mountain life."

"Yes, early 90s film, right? I saw that. Didn't one of them become an instructor and try to romance a rich girl?"

"Yes….." Eva said slowly. "But in real life the instructors should not be allowed to do such things. At least not the ones I know."

"Wait a minute," Tom said. "There was another film like that. Dumb and Dumber. Didn't that have two guys who go to Aspen and try to date a rich girl?"

"Again, yes……," Eva said. "But that did not turn out well for those guys either, I think, so you can see how that is a completely bad idea, right?"

"Yes indeed," Tom said.

"Moving on in the ski film genre," Eva said. "How do you like the Warren Miller documentary films of extreme skiing?"

"You mean those guys jumping off huge cliffs and skiing through narrow chutes only inches from jagged rocks?"

"Yes, and the girls doing that."

"Exciting and slightly crazy," Tom said. "I don't care for the hard rock music that plays with those films. Sometimes I put on classical music and just watch the visuals of those films."

"You are such a rebel."

"What I like more are the Youtube videos of a professional French skier named Candide Thovex," Tom said. "I remember one where he set up a special run where he went through a snow tunnel then through a barn and jumped over a road and onto a lake. And another where he was summer skiing down a desert sand dune, down the Great Wall of China, in a rainforest and then surfing an ocean wave on his skis."

"I've seen that. He's incredible."

Eva said she also liked to browse the Web for ski videos, especially those that seem outdated from old clothing and skiing styles.

"There's a cute music video from the 1980s with John Denver and friends skiing in Austria while John sings Dancing With the Mountains. The skiers are wearing bright one piece suits and doing ballet moves, spinning around with legs extended. It's fun to watch," she said.

Eva also mentioned the trend of teen ski comedy films around the early 1990s, including ones called Ski School, Ski Patrol, Snowboard Academy and others featuring horny or mean teens engaging in antics or contests at ski resorts.

"Not my cup of tea," Tom said. "But I am ready to head back to our own resort. Have you had enough of Aspen for today?"

"Great town, but enough for today," she said.

Red Lion Restaurant and Nightclub in Vail

10

THE SOCIAL SCENE OF YESTERYEAR

The social scene of yesterday often seems
sweeter in memory than that of today.
—Arturo Historal.

When Tom and Eva got back that night they went to have a drink with one of Eva's friends at a home in the Lionshead area of central Vail.

When they arrived, the host seemed upset and Eva asked what was wrong.

"We've been in a dither all day," the friend said. "A mountain lion got our neighbor's dog this morning at 6 a.m."

Tom's ears perked up. "Are you serious?"

"Quite," she said. "They let their spaniel out at 6 a.m. and a mountain lion got it, right here in town. Our neighbor heard it. When he couldn't find his dog, named Mogul, he called Eagle County Animal Control officers, who found the remains of the dog under the deck where a lion was spotted. The lion ran away into the residential area."

"That's awful," Tom said.

Eva said "But it's part of living in the mountains."

Eva turned to the host and said "Catherine, tell my friend Tom about the early days of Vail."

Catherine's face lit up. "There are so many stories. I've been here since almost the beginning as the buildings and first homes went up. Donovan's bar was the first hangout. Everybody went there. And then people like Ann Taylor, the fashion designer, moved here. Ann was a friend of mine and she spent winters here."

"I've heard of her," Tom said.

"Oh honey," Catherine said, putting her hand on Tom's arm. "Ann's house was the center of Vail's social scene. When you entered her French-country style home, you walked down a long hallway that was a showcase for her furs that were hanging on the wall. She was born into wealth in the East. She was a model who launched her own clothing line. When she was on the cover of Harper's Bazaar in 1946 she was flooded with orders. In 1963 she and her husband built a house here in Vail as they were one of the first investors. They had famous people like Gregory Peck and Truman Capote here for the most fabulous dinner parties."

"Did she ski,?" Tom asked.

"Oh yes, honey. She skied in the morning with her instructor and she often wore a bright yellow fur coat. Can you imagine that? She brought national attention to Vail when she was on the cover of Life magazine in 1965 on the Vail slopes wearing a Greek infantryman outfit. She was a hoot. She died in 2007."

"Is her home still there?" Tom asked.

"No. Someone bought it for $7.5 million and tore it down to build a bigger contemporary home of 12,000 square feet and a pool. Honey, you can read all this in the Vail—Beaver Creek magazine there on my coffee table. And you know President Gerald Ford had a house in Beaver Creek, right?"

"Yes, but the 60s and 70s were before my time," Tom said. "My memories of skiing are from the 1980s, but I do remember seeing a 1978 TV commercial with a cute blonde girl who skied into view and said into the camera 'Hi! I'm Suzy Chapstick!'"

"Oh sure, honey, that was the time of one piece Bogner suits, all bright and tight. It was so much fun. In fact, those onesies in neon colors have been back in the catalogs. It's so retro, don't you know? But now the suits have a pocket for your cell phone and a hood that will fit around helmets. I just love to see a man in a blue and yellow onesie on the hill! Even though I'm 87, I still flirt with the men when I'm skiing, unless my arthritis is really bothering me."

Tom patted Catherine on the leg and said. "You are a charmer." His phone rang and Tom excused himself from the conversation. It was his ski school supervisor calling.

"Tom. This is John at the school. Can you do your first class tomorrow morning, 9 a.m. It is four kids, about age 10, they are beginners but not first day learners. Just take them on some greens work on turns and stability."

"Yes, I'm ready!" Tom said.

Tom was up early the next morning and put on his blue instructor's outfit. At 8:30 he was at the meeting site in Lionshead to meet the children. All four were from the same family. The parents said goodbye as Tom and the kids got on a gondola and headed up the mountain. The four boys were 9, 10, 11 and 12.

"Where are you boys from?" Tom asked.

"Chicago," said the nine year old.

"Are you good skiers?"

"We kick ass," said the cocky 12 year old.

"So you guys are beyond the snowplow technique?"

"Way beyond the pizza stance, dude," said the 12 year old.

"Call me Mr. Woods, okay boys?," Tom said. "Alright, let's review the three basic stages of skiing as we're riding up: the beginner, the intermediate and advanced. Beginners put their skis in a V shape, with the front tips of the skis together, also called the snowplow, wedge or the pizza. To turn left, you push down hard on the right ski and that will push your body to the left. Turns slow you down. If you want to go faster, aim both skis straight down the hill in the French fries position."

"That's a stupid name," the 12 year old said.

Tom ignored his comment. "Okay. Do any of you know what the intermediate technique is called?"

The 10 year old said "Stem Christie."

"Right. That is where you start using both feet when you turn. You are still in the pizza shape, but to turn left, for example, when you push down on the right ski you also pick up your left ski and put it down next to the right ski, so you move through the turn with both skis together. Then you go back into the pizza, and do it again."

"That's where I'm at," said two of the boys.

"Good," Tom said. "Then the advanced method is called parallel, which means keeping both skis close together all the time. In this, you can still make turns with pressure on mostly one foot, but the other foot stays close alongside."

"And it looks really cool," said the 12 year old.

"Oh, is that the most important thing, to look cool?" Tom asked.

"No," said the two youngest boys in unison. "Safety is most important."

"I wish everybody felt that way," Tom said.

The group was nearing the end of the ride and Tom told them to check that they did not leave anything behind as they exited the gondola. The boys then all snapped their boots into their bindings like young pros, and were ready to go down a run.

"Follow me in some turns," Tom said. He moved down an easy run doing pizza turns and then Stem Christie turns and looking behind him at the boys. They were imitating his movements well except the 12-year old was jerking through parallel turns, skidding his skis sideways.

Tom stopped and the boys stopped beside him.

The 10 year old pointed at the 12 year old and said "He's trying to show off!"

The 12 year old said "Shut your pie hole or I'll pound your face."

"Easy boys," Tom said. "Let's all just work on some stem turns and when you start your turn I want you to squat down into it, really bend those knees."

They did a few more turns and looked more stable and in control as they stopped behind Tom.

"Okay," Tom said. "Now, I want to tell you about attitude. In skiing, you should not be afraid of the mountain. You can control yourself. You know how to stop, so there's no need for fear. You are a lion. This is your jungle. Now I want to hear you lions growl during every turn."

The 12 year old rolled his eyes at Tom.

"Humor me," Tom said to him.

As they followed Tom down the run, he growled in each turn and the boys followed, growling and laughing. On the next ride up, Tom said "Okay, now this time let's do airplane turns. When we start into a turn, I want you to put your arms out to your sides like airplane wings and then lean your body into the turn like an airplane making a turn in the sky. "

As they went down the next run the boys made airplane sounds with each turn as they followed behind Tom.

"Can you feel that airplane banking into the turn?" Tom yelled as they made serpentine turns down the run.

"Yeah," the boys said in unison.

As the lesson came to a close, they headed to the bottom and met the boys' parents.

"How did my boys do?" the father asked.

"Excellent," Tom said. "They are steady beginners to intermediates, progressing well in turns and control."

"Did you boys have fun?," the father asked.

The younger boys made a loud chorus of growls.

"This is our jungle!" they said.

Tom explained the growling to the parents, and the father smiled and reached in his pocket and handed Tom several bills of money.

"My first tip," Tom said. "I may just frame this."

Tom skied the rest of the day on his own and then at 3 p.m. slung his skiis over his shoulder and walked down from Gondola one and decided to stop in the Red Lion bar for a drink with other instructors he heard would be there. Several were lined up at the bar, still wearing their blue instructor outfits.

Tom knew only one at the bar and was introduced to several others, including a Frenchman named Jean-Luc.

"Pleased to meet you," said the Frenchman in a crisp accent. Tom judged him to be in his 50s, with sharp features and a thin neatly-trimmed gray beard. He looked every bit the suave European.

"How long have you been teaching in Vail," Tom asked.

"Oh, this is my first season," Jean-Luc said. "I'm from Chamonix and my American students there told me so much about Vail that I wanted to come see for myself." He paused and then continued "I also wanted to come while I still could. Before your president shuts down all work visas from abroad."

"Yes, we are in an interesting time," Tom said.

"Indeed, do you know that most Europeans think America has gone crazy? It seems only a few years ago you elected your first Black president, a young liberal who engaged with the whole world, then you elect a white billionaire who insults everyone and tries to close your borders to immigration and pulls out of treaties that were carefully crafted. What is going on in America?"

"It's a politically divided country."

"But don't you realize that the world looks to America for stability and vision and leadership?"

Tom was jarred by the abrupt comments from someone he just met.

"I do realize that," Tom said. "But there are different views of how to provide stability and leadership."

"Well, I am only telling you what many Europeans think. Let's drink to different views, no matter how insane they may be!," the Frenchman said. Tom ordered a beer and toasted with Jean-Luc.

A young instructor in his twenties at the bar entered the discussion and said "That's one thing I love about instructing. You can leave politics out of it completely."

"Oh not true," said Jean-Luc. "I often have clients who want to talk politics. French or European Union politics, but almost always America comes into the conversation, and one has to be careful not to offend the client. You have to feel them out and keep your knees bent through the bumps of the conversation."

"How is the Apres-ski scene in Chamonix?" Tom asked.

"The best. You do know that 'Apres' means 'after' in French, don't you?

"Yes indeed."

"We have many bars, restaurants and a fine casino. My favorite place is the bar Chambre Neuf, with live bands and the crowd dances on tables, especially when happy hour starts at 8 p.m. And of course Cortina in Italy is one of the most amazing resorts and Apres places in all of Europe."

"I try to stay off tables," Tom said.

"And the ladies are so very fine and willing. After all, they are on holiday and that is what one does on holiday."

"Are you married? Have children?"

"Never married," the Frenchman said. "But children? Yes a few."

The obvious questions crossed Tom's mind, but he let them go in favor of a new direction.

"I've never skied in Europe," Tom said. "How is it different than in America?"

The small group of instructors all laughed at the question.

"Tres bien," Jean-Luc said. "First of all, it is more about the whole experience, not just the skiing. Apres is all day. We may have a wine break at 11 a.m. The chairlift queues in Europe are more of a chaos, with people pushing to get to the front of the line. And on the mountains, there is what we call 'on-piste' area that is patrolled, and there is off-piste where you can ski long trails from town to town and different resorts. It is like out of bounds areas in the U.S. And of course, skiing is generally cheaper in Europe than in the states."

"Well," Tom said, "As a naive American and a book lover, I think of the author Ernest Hemingway when I think of skiing Europe."

"Yes, he wrote about skiing Austria in A Moveable Feast. He went off-piste and high and went from hut to hut. He wrote of skiing the glaciers, leaning into the speed, dropping forever in powder. He called it better than flying. I think he was right."

After an hour at the Red Lion, Tom left and his cell phone rang a few minutes later and his ski school supervisor gave another assignment.

"Are you free for a one hour private lesson at 1 p.m. tomorrow?"

"Sure."

"This is a 62 year old female, a beginner to intermediate skier who wants to work on bumps. Her name is Brianne Johnson. Look for a lady in a white outfit at the meeting place."

"Sounds good to me," Tom said.

11

THE BUNNY AND THE BILLIONAIRE

We never meet people by accident. Unless a snow

snake trips you on a black run. I hate that.

—Sven LaTrip.

At 1 p.m. Tom skied up to the ski school meeting location and looked for Mrs. Johnson. A young woman stood nearby holding her skis in a white outfit, but nobody in their 60s was near. Tom walked to the young woman.

"Excuse me. Would you be Brianne Johnson?," he said.

"Yes, that's me."

Tom shook his head and said "My information was that you were a 62 year old female."

"Well, not quite yet. I'm 32," she said. "Someone must have heard me wrong when I made the reservation."

"Yes, I would say so, Miss Johnson," he said.

"Please call me Bri."

Tom shook her hand and said "Call me Tom. My information says you're an intermediate skier and want to work on bumps today, is that correct?"

"Yes, exactly," she said.

"Well, we can do that. The snow is good on the bump runs today."

As they rode up the chair Tom learned that Bri was from New York, was single and with a group of relatives in Vail for two weeks. Tom and Bri did the silent evaluation of each other as they rode up, looking at each other's appearance, clothes and equipment as they talked to get the brief background of each other. They enjoyed the "chairlift check-out," asking where someone was from and what kind of work they do as they made small talk and sized up the other person for attractive-ness and economic station in life, all the while dangling in the sky and sometimes fumbling to check their cell phone for messages.

They exited the chair, put their skis on and found a nice run with varied mogul sizes and shapes. As they stood at the top of a bump field that looked like perfectly shaped ice cream scoops laid on a white sheet, Tom said "Do you know what makes moguls?"

"I think so," Bri said. "When skiers turn on steep slopes their skis push the snow into mounds, and the more people that turn in the same place, the bigger the mound and deeper the ruts get."

"Right," Tom said. "On flat runs, the grooming machines can flat-ten the bumps, but not so much on steep slopes. Well, where do you like to turn on bumps, on the tops or down in the troughs?"

"I like to be on top," she said as she smiled an innocent smile at him. "And I go slow."

"Okay. Let's go down a straight line in front of us, turning on the tops at a slow and controlled speed. I'll watch your technique and then make some suggestions."

Tom went first, smoothly gliding through the mogul field, turning on the tops and sliding down the sides of the moguls, skis parallel and feet moving independently. He stopped and watched as Bri followed his line across the bumps almost exactly.

"You're very good," he said. "Go on ahead and I'll watch."

As Tom watched, Bri made smooth sharp parallel turns on the tops of the moguls, losing balance only once and recovering quickly, as she floated up and down.

"You've got it," Tom said. "I would suggest a couple things. Keep thinking of your legs as shock absorbers, coiling and uncoiling, but keep your upper body still. Turn with your feet, but not twisting your upper body."

"Got it," she said.

As Tom and Bri reached the bottom of the run, they loaded into Gondola 1 for another trip uphill. Two other couples climbed in the cabin also and began laughing as they pulled out a ski run map.

"Yep, the run called Ben's Face is right under this gondola," said one of the young men.

"Oh no," said the other young man. "I can hear the jokes aimed at me already."

"Oh stop, Ben," said one of the young women. "We would not make jokes about skiing on your face."

"I would," said the other girl. "Is it bumpy on Ben's face?"

"Yes," Ben said. "But don't be falling on my face."

The girl sitting next to Ben hugged him and said "Right! Nobody but me can fall on Ben's face."

The foursome laughed, and Tom winked at Bri. The foursome continued joking.

"And there's no stopping to pee on Ben's face. That would be disrespectful," the other young man said.

Tom joined in. "My student and I just came down on Ben's Face. It was well groomed and handsome."

"Well thank you, Mr. Instructor," Ben said, after noticing Tom's blue uniform. "What's the best way to ski it?"

Tom said "You can ski a line straight down or you can zig zag all over. But do keep your knees bent for stability when you're on Ben's face."

The group laughed loudly. Ben's girlfriend leaned over and kissed his cheek. "It's a nice face," she said.

As the group departed the gondola, Tom and Bri headed for a near-by run with well-spaced trees.

"So what's your best advice for skiing in trees?" Bri asked.

"First, not to hit any."

"Brilliant," she said.

"Well, actually I think of first importance is picking your route well as you move along, looking for safe wide places to turn and hidden obstacles and keeping an eye on where you may exit the trees. Then go slow and do short sharp turns to stay in control. Then relax and just enjoy flowing through the forest. Stop occasionally and look at the trees and sky and enjoy the solitude. "

"That's a beautiful description," she said. "But what if you want to go as fast as you can, cranking it to your favorite head-banging music, dodging by inches a violent death-by-tree impact every second, just so you can live on the razor's edge?"

Tom frowned. "As an instructor and adult, I can not recommend that," he said.

"Just a thought," she said.

"Well, why don't you lead through these trees and I'll follow. Show me your style."

Bri dropped into the trees and moved confidently through, turning in short steps, keeping a straight line and ducking down as branches scraped the top of her helmet. Her route varied between untracked powder and rutted spots where many had been before. In a wide area still in the forest, she pulled to a stop.

"Very smooth, Bri, nice job," Tom said.

"Thanks."

"You do like to take chances with the branches though, don't you?"

"Sometimes, yes, chances with branches."

Tom took a moment to advise her of other dangers in the trees: Hidden logs. Deceptive snow that can cover a small creek. Ground-level branches lurking under snow. Even the occasional deer or moose that suddenly appear in a skier's path.

"Few things would be more unpleasant that skiing broadside into a moose," he said. "They are not friendly."

"I'll keep that in mind."

As they rode back up the gondola, Bri asked Tom what he did for a living besides teaching skiing. He explained about defense law.

"Well, my uncle is a fairly well-known defense lawyer," she said. "Edward Talbot of the Prison Justice Project. He works to get innocent people out of jail."

"I met him briefly at a conference years ago. He's amazing. He's famous."

Bri explained that the uncle was in Vail with her family.

"Would you like to meet him again? We are having a large dinner party tonight in Beaver Creek with several guests. Would you come as my guest?"

Tom hesitated.

"It's not a date," she said. "You're a guest there to meet my uncle. And there will also be other local leaders. You could get connections in to possibly practice law in Vail."

Tom thought about it. "I would love to come." Bri gave him the address, time and her phone number.

• • • • • • •

At 6 p.m. that night, Tom drove to the exclusive Arrowhead subdivision next to the Beaver Creek ski resort. A guard at the gate to the subdivision let Tom pass when Tom's name showed up on a guest list.

Tom thought about what kind of dinner party it might be. As he drove up a winding road on a hillside and pulled up to the address he found a sprawling stone home that looked like a golf clubhouse. Bronze deer and elk statues stood in the front yard. A valet parked his Range Rover and Tom proceeded into the lobby where Bri met him. He wore a black suit and silver tie.

"You dress up nicely," she said.

Tom stopped and looked at her. She was stunning in a white dress with black hair pulled up and flashing blue eyes.

"And so do you," he said. "Who's house is this?"

"My father's. He's a real estate developer."

Bri led Tom through a great room with massive log pillars, past a music room with a grand piano and into a bar and entertainment room.

"How many people at this party?" Tom asked.

"About 30. There's a couple of actors, authors, a pilot, a billionaire that owns a telecom business, a Congressman, a dancer, a few local officials and one very handsome ski instructor," Bri said. "That would be…you. The billionaire even has his own bodyguard here."

Tom smiled.

"Mother loves to plan these parties, but father loves them too," she said.

Bri introduced Tom to her parents and then her uncle came up to them.

"Why Tom Woods, so good to see you again!," said the attorney. "Bri told me you'd be here."

"I am quite flattered you remember me sir," Tom said.

"Nonsense, you have a fine reputation. And I saw you in the news a few weeks ago after the incident in court," he said. "I'm so glad you are okay."

"Incident?," Bri said.

"Just a scuffle with a client who went a bit out of control," Tom said.

The group walked out onto the back patio of the home and stood near a gas fire pit, a hot tub, an outdoor stone fireplace and a bronze sculpture of a skier leaning into a turn. A few feet behind the patio was a ski run leading down to a chairlift. The snow glistened brightly on the run in the moonlight of the night.

"Ski-in access, very nice," Tom said.

"Oh yes, it's all very nice, and for sale," Bri said. "Father has it on the market for $13.9 million if you are interested?"

"That's a bit out of my range," Tom said. "Why is it for sale?"

"Oh, he's always interested in building something new."

A server came by holding a tray of champagne glasses. Tom took one and asked the lady "May I ask your name?"

"Consuela."

"May I ask where you are from?"

"Mexico."

"I am Tom," he said, and shook her hand and looked her in the eye steadily.

"Why...thank you," she said.

"Thank you for being here tonight," Tom said.

A tall man approached Tom and introduced himself as a college history professor and author of American history books. The professor began asking Tom about the history and future of America's top tier ski towns and was expounding his own opinions.

"Well," the professor said, "I am quite convinced by the demographic data that some of these towns are being overbuilt in regard to the number of luxury homes and condos. The coming young generations and growing minority populations may not have any interest in snow sports or the financial ability to sustain these towns. And then where will they be, with these thousands of luxury homes sitting vacant as the heirs try to sell them?"

The professor waved his cocktail glass around, pointing at the house where they stood. "Like this massive place? Will there be enough of the wealthy one percenters or enough Saudi sheiks to buy these kinds of places in 50 years?"

"Will the world even survive 50 years?," Tom said.

"Yes, and, and….." the professor said as he grew more excited, "will there even be enough reliable snow in fifty years in these towns, or will global warming shut down this whole skiing industry? Mostly, I think it's a matter of whether skiing is on the downward trend of its life cycle. I mean it was small until it began to accelerate in popularity after World War II, around 1945 as more ski areas were developed, but then the small village lifestyle got overtaken by big corporations who built these extravagant commercial base areas of fur boutiques and luxury hotels and homes, and they succeeded in drawing wealthy visitors which helped boost the price of lift tickets and ski clothes and equipment. But how long can it last? I mean hula hoops and the Roman empire each had their day, and then, poof!, they were gone."

"Perhaps the big ski towns will change back to the small village model and will be affordable to the middle class again," Tom said.

"And perhaps elephants will sprout wings and fly someday," the professor said.

· · · · · · ·

A server came to the patio and announced that dinner was ready, so the group walked to the dining room and sat at a massive wood table with 15 seats on each side. With Bri's parents at the head of the table, Bri and Tom sat near them. A heavy-set man with gray hair sat across from them, and the man's much-younger wife sat next to him. Bri introduced them to Tom, noting the man, Mr. Anderson, was the CEO of one of the largest telecom companies in the world.

When all were seated, Bri's father welcomed the group.

"Thank you all for coming on this beautiful night in this beautiful valley," he said. "I hope we can make some new friends tonight."

A first course was served by five servers, and the CEO asked Tom what kind of work he did.

Tom hesitated and then answered "I'm a ski instructor."

Bri's father said "What is it like to be a ski instructor these days? Are they still revered with a cult status as in the early days of skiing? You know, the image of the blond, tanned expert who also romanced the ladies at night? It was such as status symbol to have your own ski instructor. I remember the Norwegian Stein Eriksen, who was called Aspen's Golden Stud."

"How subtle a moniker," Tom joked. "I know there is a feeling among some people that having your own instructor can convey status, and that some wealthy clients bring their own instructor along on vacations a long way from their home resort, all expenses paid, and the instructor goes clubbing and dining with the clients. And you can see a few instructors wearing uniforms from their home schools on those mountains far away while on a paid trip with their clients."

Bri's mother spoke up. "I know that at least in Europe, the best instructors can also get you the best tables at restaurants. They have influence. They know all the maître d's. They know the best places to go and hotels to stay in."

"Well, that would not be my specialty," Tom said.

The CEO entered the conversation. "Well, Tom, frankly I do not see the appeal of snow skiing. Let me count the things I would hate. First there's the silly clothes, including those rigid boots that you people clomp around in and the helmets and goggles that fog up. Then there's the continual danger of injury from falling or being hit by other people. Then there's the bone chilling cold and wind of winter. Golf is a much more sensible sport. It seems to me that skiers are paying to be miserable just to get up on a mountain so they can enjoy a nice view."

"Well," Tom said. "Skiing does require a bit of courage and adaptation to appreciate its many joys. I consider it a gentleman's sport. And thereby, I think it takes a gentleman to understand it."

"Young man, are you implying I am not a gentleman?"

"Not at all, sir. I don't know you."

"But I bet I know about you."

"Oh really. Do tell."

"I would surmise that you come from a middle class family. That you did poorly in college and dropped out to be a ski town bum. You probably worked in restaurants or ski shops until you decided it was better to become an instructor. So ever since then you have been stuck in that low wage job and you have no ambition to do any better in life. Your bank account is probably as empty as your imagination, and you could not succeed in a regular profession."

Bri's uncle, the defense attorney, let out a big laugh and put his hand to his mouth to hold back a bit of food that started to come out. He wiped his mouth and looked over at Tom and smiled.

Anderson continued. "I further suspect that any woman could hold your job. What do you say to that?"

Tom paused and considered. "I think you just insulted the female half of the population," Tom said. "And this also reminds me of the amazing workings of the human body. Let me explain. When we are in conversation like this, everything in your body is working together. The heart is pumping, the lungs are putting oxygen into the bloodstream, the blood pressure is regulating, the neurons in your brain are firing as thoughts are created and your throat and tongue are working together to launch audibly the precious words you have chosen to say. It's an orchestra, offering up the perfect moment for us to say things to uplift and encourage the people around us. And yet all of that effort is wasted on a bloated ego like yours, Mr. Anderson, an ego so swollen and twisted that you choose to insult people because it makes you feel like the bigger man when you can push people down below you. But instead of succeeding in trying to belittle people by your insults, your words only show that it is you who is the smaller person. And my guess is that the more you say, the smaller you'll get this evening, until eventually you will be the size of a speck of dust, and we can simply sweep you out the door and we won't give a second thought to you, which is probably the worst thing that can happen to someone like you who craves attention. But that is the long and short of it, and a dustpan is where you'll be and your money and your telecom company and your insulting behavior will be as forgotten as if they were never born."

Tom lifted his glass and had a taste of wine.

The CEO Anderson's face contorted with contempt.

Bri's uncle said "Mr. Anderson, I doubt that you know that Tom here is one of the nation's top defense attorneys. He just moved here a few weeks ago to spend an alternative time as an instructor this winter."

Anderson slammed his fist on the table and said "I could ruin you, boy."

"I doubt that," Tom said. "I've dealt with people like you. You have only limited tools at your disposal. Why waste them on a small fish like me?"

As the voices were raised, a very large man in a black suit came from another room and stood behind Tom. The CEO pointed at the big man and said to Tom: "This is my guard. With one word I could have him throw you out."

Tom stood up and faced the guard, and Tom put his hands in his pockets, and said calmly "I do hope you won't say that word. There's no need."

Bri's mother stood and said "Mr. Anderson. You should be the one to leave. You have ruined my party."

The CEO stood up from the table and stormed out with his wife and guard following behind.

Tom sat down and said to the hosts "I am so sorry for that."

"Don't be," Bri's father said. "He's a pompous ass."

"Let's get back to talking about instructors," Bri's mother said. "Do you know Adolf Hauswirth, of Gstaad, Switzerland? He taught the actress Brigitte Bardot to ski. I guess I am showing my age now!"

"I've heard of him," Tom said.

Servers brought the main course. Tom looked around the table, and Bri rubbed his arm.

"I'll tell you what I enjoy on the slopes," Bri said, "and that is guessing if a skier is single or married based on what they wear."

"Please explain," Tom said.

"Well, if it's a girl in rental equipment and jeans, she's single and there with friends and is giggling the entire time. If it's a young guy with baggy snowboard pants who smells like weed, he's single and broke. If it's a woman in a color coordinated snow suit and top of the line skis, she's married, or has been. She wants you to look her over. She may or may not be there with her husband."

"Very perceptive," Tom said.

Over the next hours Tom had a pleasant conversation and met several locals. He limited his drinks and at 10 p.m. said goodbye to all and told Bri he had to get up early the next morning. Bri asked if she could kiss him on the cheek.

"Yes, of course," he said.

She kissed him and said "I may just call the school for another lesson."

"I look forward to it," he said.

12

CONSUELA AND HER CHECKBOOK

America is a nation of immigrants. Let's
not forget that. I certainly can't.
—Chief Running Horse

When the party was over at 11 p.m., Consuela Garcia changed from her serving uniform into her street clothes and walked from the big house. She got into her small Ford Focus and drove down the mountain to her apartment in Avon, near the base of the Beaver Creek resort. She could see the ski runs in the moonlight from her parking lot, if she cared to look up at them, but she rarely did. She climbed the stairs to her second floor apartment and went in. Her husband, Manuel, was asleep on the couch. She checked on her two children and was satisfied that they were asleep in the room they shared. She went to her bedroom and set her alarm clock to 6 a.m. so she could get to her second job, as a hotel maid, by 7 a.m.

Consuela and Manuel were among the many immigrants who have settled into ski towns across America. They traveled north from their home in Mexico a few years earlier after friends told them of a better life in a place called Colorado: a place with jobs, schools where Hispanic children were welcome, clean cities and place without a constant threat of gang violence, murders and kidnappings common in Mexico.

At first they thought how to get to the United States. They had no children yet. They were young, newly married, yearning for a better life. They had unskilled jobs and barely enough money to survive.

"Do we have to use a coyote to get us across?" Consuela had asked about paying a smuggler.

"No," Manuel said. "We have jobs. We can show enough stability to get tourist visas. We can make the border agents believe we will be on vacation, intending to come back home."

And so that's what they did. They said goodbye to family and promised to send money home after the got settled. It was summer and they stayed in their car for a week until they could get into an apartment. They both got jobs in hotel and restaurant service fairly quickly. They bought false Social Security cards and green cards. And they lived in fear that they would be caught and sent back to Mexico, but the fear lessened as time went on. They learned English well and decided to start their family.

As their children were in school there in 2016, the population of Eagle County, Colorado was estimated at about 30 percent Hispanic or Latino, about 10 percent higher than across the rest of the state. Other ski areas reported similar numbers. In some hotels, the majority of workers were Hispanic.

Consuela sat on the couch with her husband sleeping beside her, and she checked her cell phone for messages. She thought about the rich white family she had been working for that night, cooking and serving food. And she thought about the rich Mexican families who also owned homes and vacationed in Vail.

There must be rich people in every country, she thought. Do they all go to other countries for vacations? She could not imagine such a life.

Manuel stirred and looked up at Consuela.

"What are you doing, just sitting in the dark?," he said.

"Thinking," she said.

"Piensa? What are you thinking?"

"I am happy. Just to be in this nice valley. To be safe. To have jobs. Our children are well. We are blessed."

"Yes we are," he said. "And this place is blessed to have our people. We work hard. We take jobs that many whites will no longer take. We do not make trouble. We work overtime. If we all left, I think maybe their tourism and construction companies would be hurt bad."

"Yes," she said.

"And I am glad I do not ski," he said. "A young guy who works at my shop broke his leg skiing yesterday. Now he cannot work. I cannot afford to be off work."

Consuela nodded agreement and began writing down a list of things she needed to get at the Mexican grocery market nearby the next day: chiles, pan dulce, Mexican candies, tamarind.

"And one day," Manuel said, "we will become legal residents. We will be able to use our own names."

"Is there snow skiing in Mexico?"

"Why do you ask that?," he said.

"I am just curious." Consuela took out her cell phone and searched online and laughed. "Yes there is. It says that in Monterreal is a small mountain resort that has snow falling regularly in December and January. It is about 90 minutes from Monterrey, and it is small by American standards."

"I'll bet this is true!," he said. "Things in America are so big. The stores, the houses, the cars."

As they went to bed, the snow was falling outside and a soft wind whistled through the trees outside their window.

Consuela said "I was thinking of the people here. So many of them are looking for, how do you say in English. Adventure or excitement. The skiing, the going fast, the buying new clothes or new houses.

Manuel said "Our adventure is watching our children play in the soccer games."

"Do you remember the time your father was kidnapped?" Consuela said. "It took all our money to get him back. We don't need any more... adventure."

In the morning, Consuela went to work and Manuel dropped off the children at their elementary school on his way to the café where he worked.

Consuela had a few minutes before her shift started at the hotel and she sat with other maids at the hotel and sipped coffee. They told stories of the hard times their relatives were having in Mexico, or how they needed money for something for themselves as they lived in the Vail Valley. They each gave a little money to one maid who was facing eviction from her apartment. She could now rest easy for one more month.

Before Consuela got up to start cleaning rooms, she opened her purse and took our her checkbook. She always kept the balance neatly written so she could know exactly how much she and Manuel had. The balance amount read $1,788. She smiled. That was after all bills were paid for this month. It was so good to know she had money. She felt rich. She felt warm. She felt secure. It was all they had, but she felt as full as if it were a million dollars. She held the checkbook to her chest for a moment and then put it back in her purse and locked the purse in a safe place. She then pushed a cart of linens down the hotel hallway toward the first room she was to clean. She hummed a little song and she was happy.

13

MONEY, CELEBRITY AND MARY JANE

Having money can be a blessing and a curse. It has saved
and destroyed lives. It's like a gun. It's power.
—Les O. Moore

That morning after the party, Tom walked to a small café alone in the village and ordered breakfast. As he waited, he took out of a small briefcase a financial portfolio statement from one of his investment accounts. It was a small bound notebook he had just received from his wealth manager. He looked first at the summary sheet to see how much the varied stocks and bonds were earning and he glanced first at the ending market value. It read $2.2 million. It was the total in the account and had stayed level there for some time. This was his conservative portfolio and was earning only four percent a year under an able manager who followed Tom's wishes to stay defensive and cautious amid volatile markets. But Tom wanted higher earnings. In a separate larger stock account from which Tom made all trades himself, he earned 10 percent the previous year. Why shouldn't this smaller account be making 10 percent too, he thought?

His risk-taking side and his cautious side began talking to each other. Tom decided to leave the conservative account in place as protection. He did not want to lose money. He'd seen greedy young investors crash and burn as they took ever higher risks for greater returns. He looked at the line items detailing the dividends, interests, sales, fees and other categories on his summary sheet. He thought how money was a trap. It sucked you into its world and constantly needed attention. It gave you glorious freedom to do as you please, but it also barked for attention. It was a gold nugget that glittered and needed protection. Money whispered in his ear, asking "How shall you use me?" and "What if you lose me?"

Tom put down the portfolio and felt frustrated that his conservative account was probably underperforming. It was leaving money on the table that he could be using to build his estate. But then he caught himself and crushed the negative thought. He was rich, secure, young, talented, smart....then he caught this line of thoughts and pulled back his ego and gave a small laugh at his thoughts so early in the morning. He put the notebook down on the café table and decided he felt very good. And secure. And confident in his ability to manage his life. And glad he had come to this valley to see what the future held for him.

A server brought him breakfast and Tom looked at the older man said "Can I ask you something really crass and touristy?"

"Sure," the man said.

"I'm new in town. Staying for at least a season. I'm wondering what celebrities live here."

"Celebrities are easy to mention," he said. "The lead singer of the heavy-metal band Metallica lives here, James Hetfield. And so does the former Olympic skater Dorothy Hamil. The actor Kelsey Grammer had a house in Bachelor Gulch. That's all public information. And we've seen Michelle Obama and her daughters here, and some reality show families walking around, but I would not recognize them if they talked to me. There are always some actors and musicians around but we tend to leave them alone."

The server continued: "My favorite story is about Elvis Presley. It was January, 1976 and Elvis decides to fly to Colorado for vacation. He stayed in Vail in a rental home. His posse of guys and their girlfriends take ski lessons, but Elvis wears a face mask outside to avoid being recognized. One of his guys is slightly injured and goes to the hospital and Elvis goes along. The injured guy shows his insurance card that has Elvis Presley Enterprises printed on it and the receptionist says 'Yeah. So where's Elvis?' Of course Elvis is still wearing this mask and he steps up to the receptionist and says 'He's here … somewhere'." The receptionist says 'And who are you?' and Elvis says 'The Lone Ranger.'

Tom finished his meal and headed to the slopes. He boarded a gondola with two young guys who smelled of marijuana. They laughed and were friendly and so Tom chatted for a minute and then asked them "What's it like to ski or ride high? I've never done it before. No judgement. I'm just curious."

"Oh man," one said. "It makes me feel tired. I'd rather have a clear head. Some guys like it but I'd rather leave it for Apres. I'm a park dog so I want to be awake when I'm trying to do spins or getting some air. One time I smoked a joint on a chairlift and ended up sitting on the lodge patio just staring at the sky for an hour."

But his buddy disagreed.

"I like to smoke some Jane before riding. It's relaxing. The only thing bad is you get the munchies big time."

The first one said "But we avoid hotboxing, which is smoking in the gondola, unless we are by ourselves."

Tom's next ride up the gondola was with three older men. As they sat and unzipped coats and took off helmets, Tom looked at the wrinkled faces and bright smiles of this group.

"That was a fine run," one said. "Good snow today."

"Yes, a fine day to break a hip," another replied.

"Oh shut up, you old fart," the first shot back. "If you don't want to follow me through the bumps, stop following me."

"Well somebody has to show you the right way to ski."

The men looked at Tom as he sat in his instructor outfit.

"How are you, young fella?" one said.

"Really good."

"Look at this young pup," the first old man said to the others about Tom. "He's a young instructor in one of the top ski resorts in the world. He looks in fine shape. His life is stretched out before him like a long highway yet to be driven. How does that feel, young man? "

"Today it feels really good. I've got aches and pains, but the road ahead looks good. Do you mind if I ask how old you fellas are?"

"Not a bit," a second man said. "I'm Bill and I'm 86. Harve here is 87, and Bob here is the baby at 81. And we will not talk one bit about our medications or our artificial knees or other crap like that."

"How young a puppy are you?" he said to Tom.

"I am 36."

"My skis are older than that."

"That explains a lot about why you ski like a dork," Harve said. "How about a snort, anyone?"

Harve took out a small flask and unscrewed it and took a swig.

"For crying out loud it's only 9 a.m.," Bill said.

Bob said "Oh, he just does that to amuse us. He only takes enough to wet this mouth."

"I don't hardly even swallow," Harve said. "I just like the taste of a little Maker's Mark in the morning."

"Are you fellas locals?," Tom asked.

"Yep. We're all engineers and moved here after we developed the atomic bomb in World War II at Los Alamos. We had to get away. To start fresh."

"That's bull," Bob said. "He lies to everyone going up the hill. We've all done different stuff and we just ski together."

"Did you say pee together?" Harve said. "I wish you hadn't said that. Now I've got to go."

"Well hang it out the window," Bob said.

"I would, but it would hit the ground and somebody would ski over it."

"That joke was young when God was in grade school," Bob said.

Tom said they were nearing the top of the ride and that he enjoyed talking with the gentlemen and hoped to see them later. He suggested a couple runs that were groomed the night before if they were looking for smooth gliding.

"My son is a groomer at Breckenridge," Harve said to Tom. "Have you ever ridden with a groomer overnight? It will give you a new perspective on skiing. He would be glad to give you a ride."

"I would love that."

Harve gave the name of his son and told Tom to call and leave a message.

"I will do that," Tom said.

• • • • • • •

By the next night Tom had connected with the groomer named Eddie and had an appointment to meet him at 11:30 p.m. to ride the midnight shift. Tom pulled into a parking lot at Breckenridge and several snow cat grooming machines were sitting near a building that Tom entered. Inside, people were getting coffee and looking at a white board with names of cat drivers and the routes they were to take that night.

"Eddie?" he said to a burly man with a beard.

"Yes, nice to meet you Tom."

"Thanks for letting me ride along," Tom said. "I'd like to know more about what you do so I can tell my students." A few minutes later they climbed into a cab of a massive snow grooming machine.

It had a huge plow on the front, tracks under the cab and machinery dragging behind.

Eddie fired up the monster's engine and turned on a two-way radio, a heater and then music on another radio. A voice crackled on the two-way directing the groomers as they headed out from the base building.

Eddie turned on the headlights and put his hand on a joystick device, in between the driver and passenger seat, that controls the cat's tracks. He pushed the stick forward and the cat began crawling straight ahead. There is no steering wheel, but the joystick provides good control and steering.

"Kind of like a big video machine controller stick?," Tom asked.

"Yeah, "Eddie said. "Some machines have two joysticks that control the cat's two tracks. To move straight ahead, push both of the joysticks forward."

"What do you call this machine?"

"This is the Beast," Eddie said. "It costs more than $200,000, they say, so I don't want to be bumping into any trees. This is the big boy, extra wide. There are smaller machines, and there is a special small one called a winch cat that we use on extremely steep slopes that is secured by a winch cable hooked to a post or tree to keep it from tipping forward and rolling over."

"That sounds like it could be a little scary."

"Yeah, it can be. Sometimes it tilts so far forward you come out of your seat and you're standing on the floor."

The Beast moved along slowly up a trail into the black night with its headlights bouncing off the snow. Eddie explained that most resorts have groomers working mainly two shifts: the swing shift from 4 p.m. to midnight and the graveyard shift from midnight to 8 a.m. When they need to groom in the middle of the day to touch up a run, the ski patrol will close the trail for safety of the skiers.

"Tell me about the corduroy. What are you actually doing to the snow?," Tom asked.

"Sure. We are trying to undo what the skiers and boarders have done in the daytime. They push snow into bumps and some areas are scraped thin. The plow blade in front breaks down bumps, then there is a tiller in the back that breaks down hard layers and mixes old snow with new. And lastly on the far back is the tiller comb, a rippled rubber mat that makes that corduroy texture of parallel lines that looks like you've raked dirt with a garden rake. It makes a smooth surface for carving good turns."

"Is there more than just one setting for all these moving parts?"

"Oh yeah. I've been doing this for 25 years, and the machine operator uses his experience to decide where and how deep to use the tiller and what areas to move snow from to fill in thin spots. You've got to know about snow depth, temperature and other factors. There's also a new grooming implement that will create a more powdery snow surface rather than the standard corduroy that has been the norm for more than thirty years."

They drove past another snow groomer who was shaping snow into a jump at a terrain park, where there were a series of snowpacked mounds for jumps and several metal rails where boarders and skiers do tricks. Eddie pointed at the different snow mound heights.

"Those can be fun to create. You really have to shape and stabilize the snow with your tractor."

Tom looked at the dark night sky and the thick trees on each side of the ski run they were riding up. He thought about this job of working solo in the dark, late into the night, running this big machine.

"Does it get lonely?" he asked.

"Sometimes, but mostly it is very cool to be farming the snow and watching when a moose or deer or a lion run across the snow in a full moon night, and your music is playing and then the sun comes up over the ridges at sunrise," he said. "A lot of us love it."

"What other ski employees love their jobs like you guys do?"

"The patrollers. Have you ever skied with one? Do you want me to hook you up with one?"

"Definitely," Tom said. "School me."

Two days later, Tom was standing in the ski patrol's facilities at Breckenridge in the mid-mountain Vista Haus lodge. He met a patroller named Anna as other patrollers were gathered to go out for the morning.

"There's a good number of women patrollers I see," Tom said.

"Yes, about 25 percent of our squad is women. Counting women and men we've got about 100 full-timers and 30-part-timers," she said.

The patrollers were suited up in the national uniform of ski patrollers: black pants, red jacket with a white cross on the jacket. As Anna and Tom headed up a chairlift, she explained what patrollers do.

"We do the first runs in the morning to check for hazards and snow condition, and we do the final sweep at night to make sure there are no stragglers left on the mountain, but in between that there is a lot. You probably know we respond to accidents and medical emergencies and that we do avalanche mitigation, but we also have areas to rope off, posts and fences to build, and chairlift towers pads to place and accident investigations to conduct."

"Tell me about the bombs," Tom said.

"After a snowstorm, most of our steepest slopes must be bombed for avalanche control. Patrollers make all the bombs. Sometimes we throw them down a slope. Sometimes they are launched by a canon-like piece of equipment called an AVA Launcher. We've also got avalanche-trained dogs to sniff out people who get buried."

She explained that patrollers carry beacons and wear heavy backpacks containing an avalanche shovel, a 10-foot probe (folded like a tent pole) and other equipment.

"What are the requirements to be a patroller?" Tom asked.

"You've got to be an expert skier and a certified Outdoor Emergency Care Technician or EMT," she said. "Towards the end of each ski season, the Patrol holds an annual hiring clinic to evaluate candidates for the next ski season. The clinic is a 2-day event to test skiing abilities, and a dry-land evaluation of the candidates' first aid skills."

Tom asked what type of first aid is given to injured skiers.

"The goal used to be just to stabilize on-hill patients, pack them into a sled and get them down to a care facility fast, but there is more care today as technology has improved. Breck patrollers can do a needle decompression of the chest wall for a collapsed lung and use an automated external defibrillator during cardiac arrest. And we can administer drugs to keep patients comfortable."

"And what are you thinking when you transport a person down on the sled?"

"I'm thinking go moderately fast but safe and don't scare the patient," she said.

"And do you guys do chairlift or gondola evacuation?"

"Oh yeah, we train for that," she said. "I heard Aspen had a chair evacuation the other day and some skier rappelled off a chair."

"That's crazy," Tom said.

"And dangerous," Anna said.

She explained that wider skis recently allowed skiers across the country access to significantly more challenging terrain, including side-country or out-of-bounds areas that were previously closed to resort visitors. Skiers are finding steeper terrain, cliffs, trees, and chutes in various snow conditions, which has expanded the terrain for which the patrol is responsible. She said that today's patroller also does more accident investigation in greater detail than in the past, including using photographs, diagrams, measurements, witness statements and electronic recordings.

14

LET'S QUARREL

The test of a man or woman's breeding is how they behave in a quarrel.
—George Bernard Shaw

va Wilson had worked the late shift at Pepi's that night and was waking up when she got a text from Tom. It had been two days since she had communicated with him. Or rather, since he had contacted her, as a gentleman is supposed to do in the early stages of a relationship, she thought, as ideas swam through her mind as she rustled about in her bed. Had he lost interest? Had he left town? Was this his pattern? She really did not know him well yet, of course, but he had worked his way into her life and her thoughts in a short time. They had a solid mutual attraction, similar interests and similar personality types, she thought. He was solid. Or at least he seemed solid. But how was a woman today to tell? People deceived. They lied. They evaded. They put on a face to get what they want.

Lawyers were trained in misdirection and twisting words, were they not? It had only been two years since her divorce from the congressman. Her heart was still bruised. She still envisioned her heart like a sack of potatoes hung from a tree branch and then fate had stepped up and severely battered the sack with a baseball bat until it dripped blood on the white snow beneath. Well, maybe that was a bit over the top, she thought. But there was no doubt her judgement was still shaky about men. She did not trust them. Yes, you could just decide to live without them, but who wants to do that?

She got up and woke Sophie up and took her to school. As she drove away from the school, her cell phone chimed to signal another text message. It was Tom. Eva hit the return call button. Tom answered and she said "Well, hello. I thought maybe you had lost interest."

Eva winced at her own words and popped herself on the forehead with her palm.

"No, not at all," Tom said. "I was just thoughtless to not call you yesterday."

Oh, this was the worst, Eva thought. How can I snipe back at an honest apologetic answer? This guy is good.

They were both silent for a moment and then Tom said "I'd like to tell you what I've been doing. I've been exploring. Can I take you to lunch?

"Sure," she said. "But why don't you cook me lunch? At your place." She enjoyed pushing him just a bit. He deserved it, she thought.

"Of course. Come at noon."

Tom picked up food that morning and prepared his kitchen about 11:30. The sun was shining through the bay windows. Sunlight bounced off the ski slopes as he watched skiers come down for a minute from his living room. He walked a few more steps back to the kitchen and turned on a burner on the stove. Then the doorbell rang. She was early, he thought as he trotted over and flung open the door.

"Surprise," said Bri Johnson. Her arms open wide with papers in one hand and a bottle of wine in the other.

"Hello." He frowned.

"I hope you don't mind that I stopped by. I just wanted to drop off a legal article that my uncle gave me to give to you."

Tom said slowly "How....did you know where I lived?"

"Oh, you know," she said. "People with money have ways of finding anybody. Daddy knows everyone in town. I'm not sure exactly how he got the address."

Tom turned off a switch inside himself. This girl had crossed the line. She was immediately out of his life. Tom did not care what her excuse was: cluelessness, arrogance, whatever. He had no interest in this kind of person.

"Excuse me, just a moment. I have to turn off a burner on the stove," he said.

As he ran back to the kitchen, Bri walked inside the condo and shut the door. She put the papers and wine on a table in the entryway and took off her fur coat. A moment later, the doorbell rang again. Tom heard it from the kitchen and knew exactly what was happening.

"Don't answer it. I'll get it," he yelled.

Bri opened the door and looked directly at Eva, as Eva looked back at Bri.

"Hello," Bri said. "Can I help you?"

"Is Tom home?"

"Tommy, there's someone here for you," Bri yelled.

Tom ran to the door.

Eva had her hands on her hips.

"Tommy?" Eva said. "I have not met your friend."

"Umm....," Tom said. "This is Brianne. She was just leaving."

"Really?," Eva said angrily. "Seems I hit some cross traffic here. Seems I arrived a bit too early for my own good. Or, maybe not."

"No, Bri came by unannounced to drop off something."

"Oh, it's Bri now. How cute a name. And how cute a girl."

Bri said "Thank you. Tommy is my instructor."

"Tommy?," Eva said. "Well, of course. I knew he would be popular as an instructor and he's wasted no time."

Eva turned and walked off. Tom walked a few steps after her and said "Eva, wait." When she did not, he let her go and walked back in the house.

Bri said "Well, clearly I've interrupted. I'll be going now."

Tom said nothing as she left.

A few minutes later Tom called Eva and it went to voicemail. He left the message: "There is no relationship with this girl. I don't know how she found my house. I'm sorry for the incident. Let's talk please." He got no return call.

That night Tom drove to Eva's condo in Avon. He rang the doorbell and when the door opened, a tall young man stood in the entryway and said "May I help you?"

The man's face immediately registered as familiar in Tom's mind as he mentally brought up photos linked to Eva. The ex-husband. Congressman Bill Wilson. The sharp cut of his jaw. The steely eyes. Tom had looked him up online after Eva had told about him.

In the next millisecond, Tom thought of the best reply. "Was Eva home?" would solicit questions, problems for her, perhaps jealousy from the man. Tom opted for a dodge.

"Domino's delivery for a large pepperoni. Is this 214 Canyon lane? I could not see address markings here."

"No, this is 211," the tall man said. "You've got no pizza."

"It's in the car to stay warm since I was unsure of the address."

"You don't look like a pizza guy."

"We got all kinds of guys."

Tom turned to walk away when Sophie stepped to the door and said "Hi Tom."

Almost a clean getaway, Tom thought.

"Um, hi Sophie."

The congressman said "A friend of Eva?"

"Yes."

"This is no problem, Tom," the congressman said. "I'm Bill. Hang on. I'll get Eva."

Oh, this guy was too nice, too smooth. And too damn tall.

Eva came to the door and said "Yes?"

Tom smiled and stepped back and said "I guess I came at the wrong time for my own good."

"You are such as smartass," Eva said. "You probably already know that is Sophie's dad."

"Yes, I looked him up online the night you told me about him. How ironic that he looks just like the actor Jimmy Stewart, who played a young congressman in Mr. Smith Goes to Washington."

"I know who Jimmy Stewart is, you creep. Don't you think I've heard that a million times in the five years we were married?"

"Oh, now you're exaggerating. You're way too young to have been married to Jimmy Stewart," Tom said.

"Such a smartass."

"Not really, Tom said. "But, let me tell you. I've found that the really smartass guys are the ones who lie and try to keep track of what lie they tell to each person. But it always comes back to bite them. So I avoid that and just tell the truth. Like about Brianna today. You can believe me or not."

Eva motioned for them to step away from the door and sit on the front step.

As they sat, she said "Actually, I do believe you. One part of me says I don't believe you, but my gut says to believe you. "

He put his hand on her knee. She put her hand on top of his.

"This is really disorienting," he said.

"How so?" she said.

"This level of low drama and reasonableness. I'm not used to it."

"Your mother?"

"Among others. Most others."

"People are crazy," she said.

He looked at her and said "Lunch tomorrow?"

"Better be damn good," she said.

15

POWDER IN THE BOWLS

Perhaps people love snow because it reminds them of
a childhood Christmas memory. Who can say?
—Evets Aksab

Maybe Eskimos have hundreds of words for different types of snow, but skiers have about five. The sweetest type is powder. The white gold. The fluffy fresh. It's soft. It's smooth. It's virginal. It's pure. It's dry, with so little water content that it is feather light and easy to ski through. Some professional skiers travel the globe to chase the powder storms in hopes of getting those few days a season of powder heaven. They know how to ski it. They swim through the fluff in a flow state of nirvana.

Then there is crud, a wet snow that has uneven surfaces with slippery patches and lumps and bumps and it's hard to turn skis in. Danger lurks in the crud. The snow snakes are coiled and ready to strike, taking down every visitor who is not vigilant and crouched and careful. Snow groomers are out all night smoothing the crud into an even surface.

Only the expert riders can come through it unscathed by reading the snow ahead in their path.

Third is crust, a crunchy top layer over powder that happens when the sun and wind have melted the top layer of powder and the cold then makes it freeze into a solid again. It's not quite ice, but a soft crust that you can break through and ride the powder underneath sometimes. But who enjoys that when you can crash and burn any minute? Crust is something you get off as soon as you can.

Fourth is ice, the mean, evil, unforgiving enemy of the recreational skier. It throws you down in a second, you can't stop, you begin skidding, you can't turn. Ski racers know how to ski it, carving their edges into its hardness, but amateurs flee from it like a child running from a tornado. The wise skier watches ahead for the shiny patches on the snow. Ice ahead. Steer around it or be ready to tuck and roll.

Finally there is slush. Where snow has started to melt and before it become a full puddle of water. It grabs your skis and holds them. It takes you from fast to slow in an instant, threatening to break your knees and ankles in the process. Beware the slush.

As Tom drove back home after lunch with Eva, snow began pouring down. They were the fattest flakes he had ever seen, and floated down slowly like cotton balls dropped from above. It made him think of a movie set where the fake snow coming down looked too big, too perfect to be real, but this night it was real. When he got home, he decided to walk through Vail Village and just look at the snow. It was a quiet storm. The wind was so low the flakes fell straight. The lights of the shops twinkled and couples walked arm in arm, occasionally stopping to look up at the slow shower of whiteness that began to pile up on their shoulders. The scene enchanted Tom and imprinted on his memory. He stopped and had a drink at Pepi's and got a text asking if he could teach a private lesson the next morning to a teen wanting to learn to ski powder in the back bowls. The forecast was for 12 inches overnight. Tom answered back that yes, he was free for a 9 a.m. lesson.

As he lay in bed that night he thought about deep powder skiing and he thought about piles of snow laying precariously on the mountainsides, and he decided to search online for stories about avalanches in the Vail area. He found one that told about the 2014 death of a grandson of one of the Vail founders in an avalanche. The story by the Vail Daily reported the accident happened in the East Vail Chutes, where 24-year-old Tony Seibert, of Vail, died in the slide. He was the grandson of Vail founder Pete Seibert. Three other skiers were injured in the avalanche that covered all of CDC — Charlie's Death Chute — in the popular East Vail Chutes side country ski area. The story said the slide broke 15 feet at the crown and ran hundreds of feet, and that the East Vail Chutes is an out-of-bounds area accessible through a gate from the lift-served area of Vail Mountain. It is popular with backcountry skiers, but was the site of eight avalanche fatalities in the last three decades.

Tom had never skied out of bounds areas where there are no lifts or ski patrol or grooming or safety checks of the snow, but the excitement of the concept intrigued him. And yet the avalanche story deeply disturbed him. Every time he had read about avalanches, he felt a primal fear about the moving slabs of snow. He understood how snowfalls create different layers depending on moisture, temperature and wind; and how a weak layer can sit upon a hardened layer and then break off in a violent cascade that sounds like thunder to those near it.

Tom was restless as he fell asleep, and he soon fell into a dream. In the twilight of the dream, he was skiing a backcountry area with new friends seeking the deepest powder. The friends had outfitted Tom with an avalanche beacon and other equipment. The group stood at the top of an untracked hillside and took a snow stability reading with their equipment, which indicated the avalanche possibility as "considerable," but not as the highest likelihood level.

"No problem for me," Tom said to the group. "I'll lead the way. I know how to be careful."

He started down the mountainside, jumping into turns and pushing the deep snow up to his waist, and hollering with excitement. He looked back and nobody was following him. They stood and watched.

About four turns down the mountain, Tom felt the snow begin to loosen under his feet, then the floor completely gave way underneath him. He felt himself slide to the ground and snow began covering him as he was swept along on his back. He yelled "Avalanche!" and remembered the advice that in an avalanche you should swim on your belly to try to reach the top of the snow. As he tumbled forward with the force of the snow hitting him on all sides, he flipped on to his belly and began dog paddling toward the surface.

For a few seconds, Tom felt like he was in water, being swept along a raging stream. Then blocks of snow seemed to crush him on his left and right. He screamed out in pain as he was pushed headlong forward. Some part of him had broken. He continued to try to swim upward, but now he could not tell which way was up. And then as fast as it started, the sliding mass slowed and stopped. Snow closed around him like cement, but he got one hand free for a moment and scooped an air pocket around his face, and then he could move no more. With one arm pinned back and one pinned forward, he thought of the image of an ancient mosquito preserved in amber, or ancient fish skeleton preserved in rock. Would this be where his end comes also?

Under the snow it was totally dark and silent. He yelled. He listened and heard no reply. A small voice in his head said "This is just a dream," but it was a far off soft voice and could not compete with the seeming reality of the moment. Then a pain hit him from somewhere below him, perhaps his hip or legs, he thought. He tried to move his legs, but could not.

What do you think about when you are trapped under snow? Regrets, survival strategies, family memories? All of those ran through his mind. He remembered reading in a story that if you could urinate while trapped under snow, do it, because a rescue dog's sense of smell is so sensitive that they can sometimes locate a buried person by that smell. He wished he could pee. He wondered how far under the surface he was. One foot? Twelve feet? He had no way of knowing. This is not like me, to get trapped, he thought. I'm always the careful person. I calculate the odds. I stay ahead of problems. This is not me.

A moment later he heard voices. He yelled. He heard voices again. A pole poked through the snow near his hand in front of his face and he grabbed it. It slipped through his glove for a moment and then he clamped a panicked grip on it. Someone tried to pull the pole up but he held onto his grip. He heard someone yell, "He's here!"

Tom heard shoveling above him and light emerged from above. A shovel hit his head gently and he was glad for it. Hands began digging out his face and he took a gulp of fresh air when the world opened up above. In a minute he was dug out. His friends tried to stand him up, but Tom's left leg was bent backwards and twisted, bone jutting out in a grisly fracture.

"This is so unlike me," he said to the people standing around. "I don't do these things."

"Well, this is a dream," one of his rescuers said.

"A what?" Tom said.

And with that, the dream evaporated and Tom woke up. He sat up in bed and found he was drenched in sweat. He remembered the dream in detail and he was glad to be alive.

· · · · · · ·

At 9 a.m. Tom was at the ski school meeting area and met a man and teenage boy for the lesson. The forecast of 12 inches was short by two. Fourteen of fresh snow sat on the mountain in a wonderland that covered the trees and buildings and ground. The man explained that his son was a good skier, advanced level, but not good in powder.

"He's ready to learn powder," the father said.

Tom introduced himself to the boy, Andrew, who agreed that today was his powder day.

The father held up a snorkel and said "You may need this. It's hard to breathe when the powder is up to your face." The son smiled and said nothing as the father embarrassed him with the silly prop.

Tom and Andrew headed up the mountain and Tom picked a groomed run first to let Andrew warm up before they went to the back bowls to swim in the powder.

"How long you been skiing?" Tom asked.

"Since I was 12, so five years," Andrew said.

"Do you feel solid on steeps and bumps?"

"Yeah, pretty good."

And indeed he was. The boy carved tight turns on the groomer, and threaded a nice path straight down the fall line of a bump section, always in control, even playing at turning in the troughs and the top of the bumps."

"Andrew," Tom said as they stopped to back up the lift, "You are very good. Better than most adults."

"Thanks. But I'm flopping all over in powder with no control."

"We'll, let's head to China Bowl and work on that," Tom said. As they rode a lift, Tom explained powder skiing.

"Here's how I think of deep powder," Tom said. "There is no hard floor to turn on, so do not use your hard pack technique of turning the ski on its edge to carve into the turn. Instead you want to keep the skis together to form one wide surface and then you float up and down in the snow like a dolphin moving up and down in water. So when we start at the top of this run, go straight into the powder for a little bit and push the skis up and down so you can get the feel of the snow compressing under skis, just bounce up and down for a minute there, then when you start into a turn, push down and bend down into your knees and let the compressing of the snow turn you and then rise up, unweighting and floating up as your legs get in position for the next turn, where you push down into that turn. There's no edging or skidding on a hard surface, just floating. That's why powder lovers describe it as like flying. It's a different feeling and rhythm."

As they exited the chair, Tom led into the start of the run. They quickly entered fresh powder up to their knees and Tom was glad to see it was not choppy or icy, just smooth and soft. He went straight and slow, bouncing his skis in exaggeration to show Andrew the compression of the snow.

"Can you feel it compressing like a soft carpet under your feet?"

"Yes," the boy, said. "It's easy to bounce."

Tom went into a left turn and did several more with Andrew behind him. The boy was wobbly but turning, and on the last turn he went face down. He got up and brushed himself off and said "I separated my skis. I could feel the snow pull one leg away from me."

"That's why we keep them together in powder," Tom said.

They continued on down a wide open bowl with no trees or people near them, enabling complete focus on the technique. The boy fell again and again.

Tom said "You're leaning back on your skis and it throws you off balance. Stand forward a bit, be right over the center for better control and balance. It feels weird at first, but lean into it."

Andrew tried correcting his errors in the last section of the run and made a few better and wobbling turns.

As they rode up the chair Tom said "You've almost got it. Just relax and don't get frustrated. It takes a few runs and sustained effort, but you've got the skills."

"Or the spills," the boy said. "Snow went down my back."

"So you got baptized a little," Tom said. "You're earning your skills. Listen, this is silly but I tell the little kids in classes to growl like a tiger at the damn mountain. It wants to eat you, but you are the tiger. You are strong. You are in control, not the snow. Snow is just lying there and you are the master. A person like you is smart and strong and ready for this. Let confidence and power rise up in your chest and your mind."

"Okay coach," Andrew said.

"Yes it's a pep talk but we all need that sometimes. Get angry but stay focused on a few key moves and it will fall into place."

They exited the chairlift and went for the second run. Andrew fell again and again. Tom watched him and saw that he boy was now over-thinking and overpowering. The boy's strength was fading in the deep snow, his energy being spent, but Tom did not say that yet.

As they rode up the chair again, Andrew sounded dejected.

"It's no good. I can't do this," he said.

"That is not true," Tom said. "In fact I see that you have almost got it. You're floating, but your body and mind have just not coordinated in the rhythm yet. Are you overthinking it?"

"I'm overthinking, but not about skiing."

"What's bothering you?"

Andrew was quiet and then said "a girl."

Tom nodded agreement and said "My girlfriend is mad at me. Really mad. She found another girl in my house, but there was nothing going on. But my girlfriend doesn't believe it, I think. She's been hurt before and she doesn't want to trust again."

"My girlfriend is.....pregnant," Andrew said.

Tom let the words sit there and then said "Do your parents know?"

"No. I just found out yesterday. They are going to be so pissed. They will say my life is ruined, and maybe it is."

"I doubt your life is ruined."

"How can you know that?"

"Because you are smart and strong and you'll figure it out. Lots of people face this and become parents very young and go on to have amazing lives."

"Well, we may not keep it," Andrew said.

"I see," Tom said. "I'm sure you'll make the best decisions for you and her."

They sat in silence for a minute and then Andrew said "It's just so hard to talk to my dad about this. He wants me to do everything perfectly. He wants me to go to medical school."

"What do you want?"

"I don't know yet."

"Well," Tom said. "One thing I've learned is that you have to be decisive and then move on the best you can. You may change course several times in your life, Andrew, but you've got to keep moving through the jungle. After all, you're a tiger, right?"

The boy smiled and they got off the chair.

"One more run," Tom said. "Now listen to me. You're going to do it this time. It's going to come together. Don't overthink it. Just float and keep your legs together and kick ass, okay? Don't watch me. Just go."

"Okay."

They moved down into the powder and Andrew went ahead. He stumbled in the first turn and almost went down. The second was better and by the third he was floating and turning smoothly. His body sank down into the frothy powder as he turned and rose up into the air as his weight lifted in slow motion before he sank down to turn again. Up and down he went halfway down the mountain with Tom behind him, smiling, watching. Andrew pulled to a stop near a small bush. He smiled broadly under his goggles and let out a yell of excitement.

"Yes," Tom said as he pulled up beside the boy. "Yes, you got it. Can you feel the rhythm, the float?"

"Absolutely! I got it. My weight is centered. I feel the compression and the lift. I got it!"

"I knew you could do it," Tom said.

They finished the run and talked going back up the lift and skied down a groomer on the front side of the mountain to end the lesson. Tom told Andrew's father how good the boy had done. The father looked at the boy and said "I knew he could do it. He can do anything he sets his mind to."

"I think you're right," Tom said.

"Good luck, Andrew," Tom said. "And remember to keep your knees bent and be decisive."

Andrew nodded and said thank you and walked away with his father.

16

THAT DANG SLANG

Slang is the language of the cool cats, the peeps in the know. You dig?
                                                    —Carrie Sanburg

L ike many sports, skiing and snowboarding have their own slang words for different aspects of their sport. Tom was listening one day in a café to a visitor to the valley who was a total non-skier. The older man was describing to his family during a meal about the slang he heard that day while they were off skiing.

"I was in a shop today and I heard two employees talking about skiing," he said. "Keep in mind that I know nothing about skiing. I did not know until today that ski areas labeled their ski runs as green for beginners, blue for intermediate and black for experts. And the only thing I remember about ski towns is the old stereotype of them as a haven for hippies who do lots of drugs. So I hear these employees talking. One asks the other 'What are your favorites?' The other guy says he likes to mix blues and blacks, with an occasional green. I think they are talking about pills. So the other guy says yeah, he's into double diamond blacks, but the white powder is the best, that he's totally addicted to that stuff. I figure he's talking about cocaine."

"Oh grandpa," said a teenager sitting next to the older man.

Grandpa continues. "So the one guy says the other day was the biggest dump of pow-pow he had ever seen here. He said the bowls were full of it. I figure he's talking in code about some crazy party he was at where bowls of stuff were set out on a table. He says he was so high on the pow that it was the best thing he'd ever done standing up. And he said that even when he was rolling, it was gnarly. The other guy says he is more of a park rat and that he loves to shred with his wood. Well I'm totally lost by their conversation, but I'm intrigued, so I ask them what is a park rat, a shredder and his wood."

"Oh grandpa!," the teenager said again.

"That's exactly what they said," the old man said. "But they explained that a park rat or a jibber is a guy who skis or snowboards in a terrain park where there are snow mounds and metal rails made for jumping and sliding off of. A shredder is a snowboarder who rides hard and shreds the snow."

"Very good grandpa," the teen said. "Do you know what a face plant and a yard sale are?"

"Uh, not in this context," Grandpa said.

"It's when you fall face down and wipe out and your skiis and poles come off and you leave stuff spread out on the ground all around you like they are spread out at a yard sale. Do you know what it means to be eating pow all day?"

"I'd say that when you've been skiing powder all day."

"Gramps, now you are catching on. You'll be fluent in ski speak in no time. You'll have no snow town cred if you can't speak the lingo with the local dirt bags. "

The teen explained that a six pack is a six person chairlift, and a freerider is someone who skis the backcountry. He said that an edge is the sharp metal vertical edge on the side of a ski or snowboard that you turn at an angle into the snow so the edge bites into snow to cause the ski to turn sharply.

A second teenager joined the conversation with the first teenager to show grandpa more.

"For example," he said, turning to the first teen. "Dude, how was the snow under that cornie?" (The teen looked at grandpa and said quickly and lowly that a cornice is an overhang of snow on a ridge).

The first teen answered: "Bro, it was champagne (that's dry powder, grandpa) and I got some nice freshies (making fresh tracks where no one has left a trail), but then it was bony (wood and rock landmines under your skis) and then bulletproof (icy snow that seems hard enough to ricochet bullets)."

"Well, me too" the second teen said. "I ran into death cookies (icy chunks of snow that cover the run) and chocolate chips (rocks) and chowder (chopped snow plus powder). But then I headed into the glades (trees) and I was weaving the sticks (skiing between narrow trees), but I caught an edge (metal edge of the ski catches on something) and I almost ate wood (hit a tree)."

"Oh yeah," replied the first teen. "I also had a gaper with me (a clueless novice) who was in big trouble in the trees. He wants to be a ripper (good skier or boarder), but he's just a bomber (going downhill too fast and out of control). So I decided it was time to come down for some Apres (French for After, meaning the after ski scene of drinking and partying)."

"Oh, I hate it when I have to ride with a spore (Stupid People on Rental Equipment)," said the second teen. "I'd much rather ride with a shore."

The first teen looked perplexed at the second and said "A shore? What's that?"

"It's a Super Hottie on Rental Equipment. I just made that up dude."

"Good one, bro!"

Grandpa and the family laughed. Tom laughed as he sat next to them listening. Grandpa saw Tom laughing and said to him "Young fella, do you understand this silliness?"

"Yes, I have to, I'm an instructor here," Tom said.

"Tell me some more terms," grandpa said, "with the explanations."

"Well okay," Tom said. "This morning I was skiing a radical line (a steep or difficult line of descent down a slope) when I had to do some checking (briefly setting an edge to reduce your speed) because the light was getting flat (when gray skies reduce the sunlight contrast on a slope, making bumps difficult to see). Luckily I was on corduroy (freshly groomed snow with a ribbed texture that resembles corduroy), but then I hit a chip (a rock) and took a serious core shot to my boards (damage to the base of a ski that cuts completely through the top layer and exposes the core.) Repair will be needed, Tom said."

"Very good. I'm following you," grandpa said. "Do a bit more."

"Okay," Tom said. "I had a class today of total bunnies (female skier novices with cute clothing). I take them out for the milk run (the first run of the day) and as we get on the lift, I ask the liftie (chairlift operator) if he's had any lift lickers today (kids who freeze their tongues on the chairlift pole). He said no and we continue on. I did some poodle turns (demonstration turns by the instructor) and the bunnies followed in my path. There was a nice dust on the crust (a light layer of fresh snow on top a hard base of snow) and we were carving some sweet turns. Then all of a sudden a bombing knuckle-dragger (a snowboarder leaning down with his knuckles to the ground) comes ripping by and he pops a helicopter (a 360 degree turn in the air off a jump) just above the head of one of my students. I report him to the patrol and they catch him and yank his pass (revoke and remove a ski pass that is worn on the jacket to allow access to the mountain). We continue on and I show the bunnies how to do the Wedeln (wiggling-hip turns down the center line, knees and feet close together) and the bunnies are feeling very cool, so it all turned out all right."

"Good story, instructor," grandpa said.

Mid-Vail lodge in the background

17

ABUSE IN THE VALLEY

I sometimes wonder why women put up with men at all.

—Evets Aksab

On a cold February morning, Consuela Gonzalez went to her third job as a housekeeping worker at a condo building. She was feeling good. She was among many undocumented workers at that company and among many more at the numerous condo buildings that rose high above the Vail valley floor, providing space to owners of timeshares and full ownership condos.

As she went in the supply room to gather housekeeping items to begin cleaning rooms, her supervisor slipped in behind her and locked the door behind him. The young man said she looked pretty today. He told an inappropriate joke and then he blocked her way as she tried to exit the supply room.

"Don't you like me, Consuela?" he said.

"I have to go," she said. "Por favor."

"Please what?" he said.

"Por favor get out of my way." She pushed past him and he touched her back as she went past.

"Until tomorrow," he said.

Consuela felt shaken as she moved down the hall with her supplies and she waited until she saw him leave before she opened a door and began cleaning a room. She did not want to get alone with him in another room. She thought about how she had heard other maids talk about how this supervisor had intimidated them and touched them. One maid had reported him to the higher management, but no action had been taken. One of the other maids had suggested they go to the police with their combined stories, but they were afraid. Afraid of losing their jobs. Afraid of being deported.

The maids left the doors open as they worked in the rooms so they would not be trapped alone. Consuela felt in her pocket for the small knife she carried for protection ever since she was a teenager. As she felt the blade, she heard a door close behind her. She turned around and the supervisor was there.

"Can I get anything for you?" he said, as he moved closer to her. "You know, if you are nice to me, I can help you in this job, to keep this job, and maybe get a raise."

She stood still.

He leaned forward and put his arms around her and kissed her.

Consuela took a step back and slapped him on the face so hard that it threw him off balance. She stepped around him and opened the door and stood in the hall by her supply cart.

He glared at her and walked off down the hall.

Consuela lifted her right hand and looked at the blade that was concealed in the palm. She did not realize she had automatically reached in her pocket and taken it out. And now both hands were shaking and her heart was racing. She went downstairs and told another maid that she was going out for a few minutes to run an errand and she would be right back if anyone was looking for her.

Consuela walked out of the building and down a Vail street past the retail shops. She looked in the windows and calmed herself. She went into an art gallery. Pictures had always calmed her. She was looking at an oil painting of spring flowers on a mountainside when another store patron walked up beside her.

"The flowers are beautiful, aren't they," he said.

"Yes."

The man looked at her and said "I think we met at a party recently at a house in Beaver Creek. You were serving and I was a guest. I asked your name and you said Consuela. I told you my name was Tom."

She looked at him and remembered the young man who had stopped and looked in her eyes that night and acknowledged her as a person.

"Yes, I remember," she said.

Tom saw her eyes were red and she had been upset.

"Are you okay?," he said.

"No," she said, sensing she could trust this stranger. "My supervisor at my housekeeping job just tried to force himself on me a few minutes ago. I had to get away so I came out for a walk."

Tom saw her uniform on under her light coat.

"Consuela, I am sorry that happened. We should have zero tolerance for that. I am a lawyer, I represent people in trouble. Maybe you should go to the police," he said.

She shook her head left and right.

"No, I will find another job," she said.

Tom looked at her and said "If I can help with any advice, I hope you will give me a call." He handed her a business card with his cell phone number on it.

"Looking at paintings always makes me feel better," Tom said. "I get lost in the colors and shapes. I wonder how the artist can create an entire world on a blank canvas."

"My father is a painter in Mexico," Consuela said. "He taught me how to look at paintings and photographs, and how the frames are important."

"Yes, they are," he said.

"This painting," she said, pointing at the flowers. "I look from the top to the bottom. I see the sky with different light. I see the mountain shapes, the flowers, the ground underneath, where the horizon line is."

Tom marveled at her and tried to imagine what this young woman's life was like in Mexico and now in America. He thought about the irony of immigrants coming to America and winding up in one of its richest areas like this valley, of finding peace but struggling still with their own poverty and the discrimination and harassment that can happen at any time.

Tom said goodbye to her and went for a drive. He drove by an art supply store and then pulled the car into a parking lot just beyond it and turned around. He went back to the store and stood looking at the rows of canvases of many sizes, the paints and brushes and other supplies.

It was time to experiment.

• • • • • • •

An hour later, Tom Woods the lawyer stood in the guest room of his condo looking at an easel with a large blank canvas, and a table with paints, brushes and a few books on how to draw and paint. Sunlight streamed in the bay window. Why had he never stood here with this intent before, he wondered. He guessed that he had never slowed down long enough to consider doing it.

Tom walked a circle around the room. He told his smart speaker to play Mozart and a light classical song began. With no drawing experience and only a few times of trying painting when he was much younger, he wondered what he could reasonably create today that would not look horrible. He thought of the impressionists who splattered paint or dripped paint on a canvas in no seeming order or design, and yet that was admired as art by many. Couldn't he do that? He thought of highly detailed portraits and knew he could not do that. Nor could he start out doing beautiful landscapes.

He thought of simple colors in lines or blocks. He stood back and loaded a thick brush with alizarin red and painted a square block of red. Next to that he did a green block and then a yellow and a blue block and on he went until his first canvas was filled. And he was not disappointed. It was simple. He had seen similar things in homes and galleries as contemporary art. He thought about doing a canvas of leaves. Surely he could draw a small picture of leaves laying on top each other, and then paint each leaf over in complimentary fall colors.

Perhaps he would read the drawing book tonight and sketch that out. And as he thought of it, Tom the trial lawyer seemed very far away, and Tom Woods the ski instructor seemed closer at hand, and new versions of himself seemed to be just ahead, and he wondered where he was going. He told his speaker to stop the Mozart stream. He told it to play the song "A Change Would Do You Good," by Sheryl Crow. And he smiled and he reached in his pocket and took out the bullet and set it on his painting table next to the cerulean blue and ochre yellow.

He opened a book on painting and read about famous politicians who became amateur painters: Winston Churchill painted landscapes to help avoid depression, George W. Bush painted portraits, and Adolf Hitler painted serene outdoor scenes in his early years. He read that Hitler applied to and was rejected twice by the Academy of Fine Arts in Vienna. Dwight D. Eisenhower received a painting kit from a friend and went on to create more than 250 paintings.

What is appealing about painting?, he wondered.

Why was he drawn to it at this time of life?

He read on about actors and musicians painting in his own era: Jim Carrey, Sylvester Stallone, Joni Mitchell, Bob Dylan, Pierce Brosnan and Viggo Mortensen.

Does an artistic urge in one area lead to the same urge to create in other areas?

Tom set up another blank canvas. He stepped back and looked at it. His mind filled with ideas.

He thought of Picasso with his paintings of twisting torsos and three breasted women. He thought of Vincent's Starry Night with its swirling lights in the sky above a tiny village. Perhaps Van Gogh tried to imagine the swirling stars or perhaps in his illness he actually saw lights swirling in the heavens, Tom thought. What does it mean to think outside the normal for your time?

Tom asked his smart speaker to tell the types of painting styles.

"Abstract, Contemporary, American Realism," the female computerized voice said. "Folk, Art Deco, Art Nouveau, Pop Art, Classical, Academic, Neoclassical, Expressionism, Cubism, Realism......"

"Stop, stop....." Tom said. His thoughts were spinning.

"I'm not painting three breasted women or pop art soup cans at this point," he said aloud to himself.

He recalled seeing a movie about abstract painter Jackson Pollock, famed for drip style paintings that looked like swirling tangles of spaghetti in varied colors that Pollock created as he stood above the canvas dripping paint.

"I don't understand the appeal, but maybe I could imitate that," Tom said. He put the canvas on the floor and swirled a circle of dripping yellow on it, then overlapped a red and blue and black and green. Was this only about movement or was it to represent something in nature? He stood back and looked at it and nothing came to mind. Perhaps if it was all on a purple background?

Tom decided to go out and walk around Vail to look at art. He looked at the outdoor art as he walked. Sculptures of dancing children, a bronze bear, a bronze skier near Gondola One. Perhaps he should try sculpture?

He stopped into one of the large art galleries. He marveled at the detail of traditional landscapes with misty mountains and he fell in love with contemporary stylish scenes of skiers painted in a storm of colors in dot and drip painting styles. It looked to him as though many had a traditional scene that was overlaid with thin drip lines.

"How is the art business today?," Tom asked the employee behind the desk. "Do traditional landscapes still sell?"

"Somewhat," the employee said. "But the trend is to the contemporary."

"And is the market strong for sales in art galleries or has it been hurt by online sales?"

"People still love to see art in person," the employee said. "But in recent years we have lost business to art festivals. A lot gets sold in summer art festivals."

Tom walked on. He thought of his life now as a blank canvas. Or perhaps a collage where one-third had been painted and the rest still blank for him to fill. How would he fill it? Traditional scenes, new impressionism? He was not sure yet, but he was excited to see how the canvas would be filled.

At 10 a.m. Tom went home and got into his running clothes. He went for an hour run through the streets of Vail from east to west and returned home exhausted. He showered and got ready for lunch with Eva.

18

A HOSPITAL VISIT IN FEBRUARY

When a woman is talking to you, listen to what she says with her eyes.
—Victor Hugo

At noon the doorbell rang and Tom opened it to find Eva there for lunch.

"Is it safe to come in?" she said.

"Completely," he said. "Lunch is even ready."

She looked closer at Tom and he had paint on his shirt and a spot on his hair.

"Been painting a wall?" she said.

"Not exactly," he said. And as lunch progressed he told her about his new effort.

"It's good to try new things," she said. "Sophie loves to paint. Children have such a curiosity and freedom and lack of fear to try new crafts and sports. It's like they don't fear failure or rejection or compare themselves to painters they have seen. I guess we don't fall into those traps until we get a bit older."

The lunch went well and Tom was feeling good about it. He left to teach a class and Eva left for work at Pepi's. At 9 that night, Tom's cell phone rang and a friend of Eva's told Tom that he may want to know that Sophie had been in an accident and was in Vail Valley Medical Center's emergency room. He drove there and went in to find Eva. He found Eva standing with her ex-husband in the waiting room.

"Is she okay? What happened?" he said.

Eva said coldly to Tom "She's got a broken arm. You did not need to come."

Tom could sense that something had changed between them. He pulled her aside and asked if it was because the ex-husband was there.

"No," Eva said. "We just don't need you."

Tom asked if he could go in the room to see Sophie.

"Yes, for just a minute," Eva said.

He went into the room where a nurse was bandaging Sophie's arm and putting it in a sling.

"What happened?" he asked.

Sophie smiled at him. "I fell down our stairs. It's stupid, I know."

"Why did you fall?"

"Well," she said. "Mom was upset. She was talking with me about, well, you. She was saying that we did not need someone else in our lives. That you are nice, but we were just fine the way we are. She was sniffling a little bit, and then it turned into an ugly cry. You know, where your face is all twisted up and stuff is dripping out of your nose?"

"Yep, I've seen it," Tom said.

"So I asked her what the heck she's talking about and crying about. I asked if you asked her to marry you or something. She said no, but that we were just fine, and she started walking down our stairs carrying a laundry basket and I fly down the stairs behind her and I hit the side of that basket and fall head over heels down the rest of the stairs."

"Oh, I am sorry," Tom said.

"Well, it's not your fault, as far as I can see."

"Relationships are complicated," Tom said.

"Don't I know it," Sophie said in her most grown up voice.

"I'll talk to your mom about it. Things will be okay. I'm glad you're okay."

When Tom went back into the waiting room, he told Eva that Sophie had explained.

"I'll call you tomorrow," he said.

"No need. She will be fine," Eva said.

When Tom called the next day, his call went to Eva's voice mail. He left a message but Eva did not call back that day. Or the next. He texted her and got no reply. The next day he went to her condo and knocked on the door and looked in the windows, but no one appeared home. He knocked on a neighbor's door and the neighbor answered and said she believed Eva and Sophie were gone on a trip. Tom decided to let it go for a few days, which turned into a few weeks and February began to pass quickly.

One day Tom made a trip to Denver with an older fellow instructor named John to have dinner and meet friends. As they drove down the mountains and then foothills, the instructor pointed to the south side of Interstate 70 and showed a spot where a small ski area used to be right next to the highway in the Genesee area only a few miles from Denver.

"It was called Arapahoe East and operated from 1972 to 1984 and was owned by people who owned Arapahoe Basin Ski Area further west," John said. "It had night skiing and a base lodge and only 600 vertical feet, but it was very popular because it was so close to Denver."

Tom looked where the few wide ski runs had been located and saw horses walking on the hillside and a barn below.

"I would not have guessed a ski area was there," Tom said. "It looks like a natural hillside now."

"Most people drive right by it and don't know," John said.

John explained that Colorado had many former ski area sites. Some closed due to lack of revenue or other business problems, and some in the lower elevations could not get enough consistent snowfall.

A big former area was Berthoud Pass Ski Area, that operated from 1937 to 2001 about 57 miles northwest of Denver. As a very popular area and high up at 12,000 feet, it had at least 30 instructors and was the first area to allow snowboarding on the slopes in Colorado, John said. There was also a small ski area at Pikes Peak from 1939 to 1984 and a little area nearby with a double chairlift beside the famous Broadmoor Hotel in Colorado Springs.

"There are websites that tell all about these areas with photos and stories," John said. "I find the history quite interesting. What was popular, what did not last, even some that go out of business and sit dormant and are then resurrected."

"I've got a relationship with a lady that is sitting dormant right now," Tom said. "I wonder if it will be resurrected."

A few minutes later John said they were about to drive by an indoor skiing facility in Denver, and did Tom want to see it.

"Yes, I've never seen one," Tom said.

Inside they saw a slanted ramp with a moving floor on it, similar to a walking treadmill. Children were learning to ski and snowboard on it, standing with skis in one spot and moving their feet as the floor moved beneath them and they watched themselves on a mirror in front of the ramp.

"This is great for adults too to see how you are moving and get the muscle memory," John said.

"So indoor skiing is not on snow?" Tom asked.

"Well not at this facility," John said, "but across the world there are huge indoor skiing businesses with snow-making in climate-controlled buildings. Imagine riding a chairlift indoors and skiing down real snow inside a dome while it is summer outside. Some of the biggest domes are in Dubai, in the Middle East, and in Japan. But there are also these resorts in China, France, Norway, Russia, five of them in England, and other countries. It's like being in a snow globe. The one in Dubai has five runs. It's like artificial winter and a good place to introduce people to skiing."

Tom said, "Well there are indoor skating rinks, so why not indoor skiing?"

"Exactly," John said.

19

A LESSON GOES SOUTH AND A LADY RETURNS

When a ski lesson starts to really go downhill, so to
speak, I start thinking of what's for dinner.
— instructor Sven LaTrip.

March is a green and muddy month in the lowlands, but at Colorado's ski areas, it can be the whitest and best month of all winter. Spring Break week brings families, college students and high schoolers in droves. The hotels fill, the restaurants are overflowing, the parking lots are full and the ski school runs at full speed.

Tom taught children and families. One morning a storm blew in as he rode with a family of four up the gondola for a lesson.

"Where are you from?" he asked the father.

"Iowa," the father said. "This is our annual trip."

The mother and father were seated next to Tom. Their children, a boy of 12 and girl of 14, were seated across from Tom, sending texts on their cell phones. Tom said he understood the family was comprised of beginner and intermediate skiers and wanted instruction to work on turns.

"Is your equipment okay, comfortable?" Tom asked. The father said yes.

"It's always a good idea to check your rental equipment and your clothes from toes to top of your head before you go out for a day," Tom said. "Get in and out of your boots and bindings. Check that you have enough clothing layers to be warm and that your coat is loaded with all the little things you need: sunblock, money, wallet, Kleenex. And take a face mask or a scarf for cold days. And that your helmet and goggles fit well."

None of the family answered, but looked out the windows and checked their cell phones. Then the father said "I don't think we'll need sunblock today."

A stiff wind came up and snow blew sideways as they exited the gondola and began down a beginner run.

The family of four went into the pizza stance and made wobbly turns as they followed Tom. Then the boy gained speed and bumped into his sister from the side, knocking her over.

"Hey watch out," she said.

"You watch out," he snapped back.

Then the mother fell on a bump and needed help getting up, so the father was closest and slid over to her but lost control and ran over her, which sent him tumbling. Tom could see the lesson and family fun was going downhill. Once they were up again, he continued on demonstrating how to edge a turn to reduce speed, but the family was not doing well. Then the girl fell and then the father fell again.

"This snow is too thick. Let's go on a smoother packed run," the father said.

Tom explained that the wind and heavy traffic on all the greens was moving snow into thick spots on all the runs. The mother said "Well then, can we go where it's not snowing or windy?" Tom looked at the sky and then at her and thought "Are you kidding?"

Soon the teenagers fell again and again, and the girl screamed at the boy "I hate you." The boy screamed back "I hate you more."

The girl screamed at her parents "I am so done with this stupid sport. I can't stay up. My feet hurt."

The boy screamed at his parents "My face is freezing. My goggles are fogged. I want to go in, right now!"

Tom asked if they had face masks or scarves. None did.

The girl took off her skis and started walking downhill. The boy saw her and took off his skis and started walking behind her. Other skiers were flying by to their left and right on the crowded run. Tom skied up behind the teens and told them to move off to the right side and walk by the trees.

The mother skied slowly in the wedge up to Tom and said "I'm sorry. They are not normally like this."

Tom let them walk a short distance to the next lift and rode back up. The family caught the gondola down and ended their lesson.

Tom wondered if surf instructors had days like that on the water and he decided that family drama was probably a common occurrence in all sports.

By the afternoon that day the sky cleared and Tom met another young family at 1 p.m. to ski beginner runs. The parents and three children were a complete opposite of his morning lesson. The children put their phones away and asked questions of Tom. They skied in control, watched for danger from other skiers and were thoroughly prepared.

As they rode up a chair after a run, Tom said "Can I ask how you guys are so well prepared?"

"Mom runs through a checklist with us every morning on all our equipment and clothes," a teen girl said. "And Dad talks with us about what we are going to do and how to focus before we go out to ski."

"Awesome," Tom said. Then the family asked Tom about funny things that have happened to instructors.

"Well, I have one friend who tells the best true stories about what happened to him over the years," Tom said. "He says one day he and another instructor were riding up a lift and they did not have the safety bar pulled down to hold them in. They both leaned forward to look at a pretty girl skiing by under the chair and at that moment the chair-lift stopped quickly, which sent them sliding out and falling. Luckily they were not too high up and they landed in soft snow and were not hurt, but they were pretty embarrassed. Another story of his is about the day he took his instructor's exam where you ski down the mountain and are judged on your ability by the ski school teachers. He was warming up on a run before the exam was to start and he went over a jump and did a helicopter, where you spin a 360 degree circle in the air. In the air his ski pole hit his two front teeth and knocked them out, but he carried on the rest of the day and passed his exam before he went to the dentist and got his teeth repaired."

After another run the family and Tom took another chair ride up when an extra passenger loaded onto their chair and rode up with them. She sat on the far side, four people away from Tom and listened to him talk.

The family asked where Tom was from.

"I'm from New York originally. I was a cardiologist there, but my heart was not in it, so I came west," he said.

The family laughed and the extra passenger groaned and said "That is a terrible joke and it's not even true."

Tom said "Pardon me?"

The passenger raised her goggles and Tom saw that it was Eva.

"He's a terrible liar," she said to the family. "He's from California."

Tom looked at her and said "You got new goggles and a new coat. I did not recognize you."

Eva said to the family "He's a good instructor. And quite popular with the ladies."

The family of three turned in unison to look at Tom for his response.

Tom said very slowly "Thank you for the compliment."

The father said "Were you one of his students?"

Eva said "Well, let's just say I've learned about men from him."

The teenage girl said "Oh, I see."

"No, no, no," Tom said. "We are just friends. She loves to play jokes on me, but I have not seen her in a while."

Tom changed the subject quickly and then at the end of the chair ride, he watched Eva ski away the opposite direction from the family. At the end of the lesson, Tom walked back into town and thought about Eva. He went into two art galleries along Gore Street and surveyed their collections. He then went into a small gift shop and said hello to the owner. In a brief conversation the owner said he was retiring to the East coast at the end of the season and his shop space was going to be open in the summer.

"How much is the lease?" Tom said. The owner explained details and Tom began thinking about art.

That night he researched online what is required to operate an art gallery to sell fine art. The next day he went to the condo building where he knew that Consuela had worked. He asked if she was in and before he got an answer he saw her down a hall. He walked to her and said "Good morning, Consuela. Do you remember me."

"Si," she said. "Hello Tom."

He said "I may be opening a very small art gallery here in Vail this summer. I am wondering if you would be interested in working for me there. I will need someone who speaks Spanish and knows art."

She looked perplexed at him. "Do you know about running an art gallery?"

"No, not at all," he said. "It might fail, but I think I may give it a try. Would you like to talk to me more about it?"

She looked at her housekeeping uniform and the stack of towels over her arm and said "Yes. I think I would."

He got her phone number and said "I will call you tomorrow."

As he walked away he stopped and said "We might fail, but we will keep our knees bent through the bumps."

She said "Knees bent?"

He said "I will explain later."

20

CREATING YOURSELF, AND AN APOLOGY

Life isn't about finding yourself. Life is about creating yourself.
—George Bernard Shaw

The next morning Tom sat with a cup of coffee and read the Vail Daily as the sun came up over the valley. A story told about a "grand vision" for improving the valley for the future and which included burying Interstate 70 underground in the stretch where it passes through the town of Vail. Traffic experts had been saying eventually the highway would need to be expanded from the current two lanes east and west to three lanes in each direction. Residents were talking about how much better it might be to bury the highway, opening up prime land above the highway to possibly build affordable housing or other developments. The problem was that costs to bury the highway would be very high, somewhere above $3 billion. It was suggested there could be toll sections of the highway implemented to pay for the costs.

Tom envisioned all roads in the town buried underground and even all parking lots and garages, and then eventually when cars were no longer a mode of transportation, the abandoned roads and parking structures were left to rot as history moved on. Tom walked into his painting studio and picked up his paints and began a painting of a river flowing out of green forested mountains. Into the river's current were long winding threads of greens, and blues, oranges and yellows. His phone rang and it was his dad.

"Hello Dad," he said. "How's LA?"

"Rainy today. How's Vail?"

"A bluebird day," Tom said. "But I am inside this morning, trying my hand at oil painting."

"That sounds great. I'm calling to tell you that I've moved the rest of your cases over to our associate Hal Brown. I hope that's okay with you."

"Of course, Dad, he's a great lawyer."

"Yeah but he's no Tom Woods," his father said. "It will be April soon. Have you decided to stay in Vail or come back when the skiing closes soon?"

"I have not settled that case yet. Still in negotiations… with myself," Tom said. "But you'll be the first person I tell."

His dad laughed. They talked for a few more minutes and then his father said goodbye, explaining that the business jet was waiting. He was off on another trip.

Tom put down his phone and it rang a few seconds later. He punched the speaker option and said hello as he looked at the multi-colored river taking shape on the canvas.

A voice said "Hello. This is a person calling to apologize."

Tom stopped and listened and said nothing.

"Would it be possible for you to accept an apology?" the woman's voice said.

"It depends… on who you are," he said, "and the terms of the apology."

"The terms would be unconditional surrender," Eva said. "And admission that I was wrong. I was scared. I'm still wary."

"Me too," he said. "But wary is a good thing."

Tom heard Sophie talking in the background.

"Well, if you have not moved on completely to new people or new towns, I'd like to see you," she said.

"I've not moved anywhere," he said. "I'm right here."

"How about 1 p.m. today at Gondola One for a few runs?"

"You're on," he said.

At noon Tom went up for a couple runs before he was to meet Eva. Once again the sky was a brilliant blue with clouds of white pushing across the sky. He rode a chairlift by himself and watched the clouds roll across the sky making shapes as the wind pushed them. Strands like white fingers pushed forward and then retreated back into the clouds. Two clouds formed into the shape of a running horse and then resolved into a blob a moment later. Tom's gaze dropped to the ridgeline of the Gore range and he noticed the jagged snowline, where the snow sat and where it was absent, where the mountains looked blue and where gray and where purple as the light shifted on them. His attention shifted down farther into the treetops ahead of him and he looked closer at how the treetops swayed in the breeze and some tops were thick with dark green and some thin with light green colors. Then he did the same with rocks dotting the ground and the snow, as he learned to see as an artist.

He took one run on an easy run and left his earbuds out and music silent as he totally focused on carving smooth turns. He leaned his body far to the left and then right, looping in big turns and his body was totally at ease. He thought of his colleagues in Los Angeles, making court appearances and devising strategies and advising clients and he was glad for the moment at least to be quiet and simple and free and alone with his thoughts this day.

He reached the bottom and loaded onto a chair with a middle aged lady.

"Lovely day," she said.

"Incredible."

"Local?," she said.

"Yes. For only a few months. And you?"

"Yes. For a few decades."

"What kind of work do you do?," she said.

"I'm in......transition. Was a lawyer....well, am a lawyer. Moved here and now a ski instructor."

"Like it?"

"Love it," Tom said.

"What do you do?"

"Psychologist and career counselor."

Tom laughed. "Maybe I should call you for a session."

"I'm glad to talk now if you'd like."

"Really?" Tom said. "Well, okay. I'm 36. Defense lawyer in Los Angeles. I have loved it but also had a nagging feeling for several years that I should do something else, wanted to do something else, but not sure what it was."

"So you quit and moved here?"

"Well, let's say I'm on sabbatical. I can return. It's my father's firm. I'm on the path to take it over, maybe."

"I see. Was it Dad's idea for you to become a lawyer?"

"Not at all. He never pushed. But maybe it was my desire to imitate him or please him."

"That happens all the time," she said. "And we don't even consciously realize it."

"But I've been so good at it. And I mostly liked it."

"But maybe you could be good and like something else even more. That inner voice talks to us for a reason."

"My mother is afraid I'll become a ski bum."

"I hate that term, but we still hang on to it," she said. "Are you any good at discovery?"

"Well," Tom said. "Legal discovery is the search for information you can use for your case, including evidence the other side has."

"Exactly," she said. "It's like self-discovery. I've got a lot of clients who moved here to find themselves, to use an old cliché, but it's really to be themselves. Some are young, some are old. They are all discovering a place, their talents, their desires at their specific point in life. We change, you know?"

"It's damn hard."

"You bet it is. And scary. And can be expensive. That's why so many people avoid it and settle for where they have been."

"How do you know if it's time to make a change or stay on the path?"

"It's a bunch of things: Sometimes it's the inner voice and feelings. It's easier if you clearly feel burnout or physically sick from your job or don't feel competent at it. But mostly I think, you have to do the work of discovery. Often we don't find ourselves, we make ourselves."

"And then there's deciding on an exact way ahead."

"Are you decisive and risk taking and confident?"

"Oh lady, I've got so much of those that I have to keep the ego in check."

"You'll do fine. Did you know that famous chef Julia Child wasn't cooking meals until age 36. Or that milkshake device salesman Ray Kroc founded the MacDonald's fast food franchise when he was 52?"

"Nope."

As they neared the top of the chairlift ride, she handed Tom a business card. He held out his hand to shake hers and said "I'm Tom. I'll be in to see you soon. Do you counsel relationships too?"

"Of course. That's what we're all about, in one way or another."

Tom skied another easy run to the bottom. At 1 p.m. Eva came walking up with her skis. Her hair was shorter. They talked and skied and filled each other in on what they had been doing. At 3 p.m. the sun began to sink in the west and a golden light spread across the ski runs in a glow that seemed to say the day was coming to a close. As they came down a flat area slowly toward the bottom, Eva reached out and took Tom's hand and they glided together to the base lodge to end the ski day, hand in hand. Tom realized it was the first time he had ever held hands with a woman and felt completely at home with her, as if his hand belonged there, as if their two hands were one.

As late March arrived, Tom taught many lessons to groups of children and enjoyed their simple joys at being on the mountain and the speed with which they learned. One cold day he was with a group when his phone rang. He recognized the phone number so he took the call.

"Hello," he said.

"Honey, this is your mother," the voice said coldly.

"What's wrong, mom?"

"Your father has had a heart attack. He's in intensive care. I need you and your brother to come home."

"What happened?"

"He collapsed at work today."

"Is he going to be okay?"

"I don't know."

"I will be there in a few hours," he said.

Tom took his class of children to the base lodge and got another instructor to take his place. He arranged a flight out of Eagle-Vail airport and landed in LA a few hours later and went straight to the hospital.

Scott Woods was unconscious as his sons stood at his bedside while a doctor explained that a massive blockage had damaged the heart and it could not be repaired. Scott was losing strength and was going in and out of consciousness as the time grew short, the physician said.

The sons and their mother stayed by the bedside for several hours and when Scott awoke they seized the chance to talk to him.

"Can you hear me, Dad?" Tom said.

"Yes."

"Do you know what happened?"

"Yes, I talked to the doctor when he came in. He said there was nothing effective to do."

"I love you, Dad," Tom said.

"I love you boys too, and you Iris. I am proud of you all."

"Tom?," Scott said.

"Yes, Dad."

"Whatever you do in Colorado or with the law firm, I know you'll make the right decision for you," he said.

"Thank you, Dad."

Scott Woods talked to his other son and his wife for a few minutes before closing his eyes and lapsing back into unconsciousness. A few hours later his heart rate slowed and stopped. His family gathered beside the bed and said goodbye.

Tom stayed in Los Angeles for two weeks as he helped his mother and managed his own grief. He worked with the partners at the law firm to settle the necessary business and handle the funeral, and in the late afternoons went to the beach to walk and to surf.

He paddled out on the waves and sometimes sat just looking at the horizon and the shoreline and felt the water rise and fall underneath him. He loved the ocean and the hills in the distance. When a wave came up underneath him he rose up on the board and gripped it with his feet and felt the sway of the water as he moved the board into looping turns left and right.

Tom's mother had two sisters nearby and one from afar that moved in to live with Iris. She began adjusting and leaning on her sisters, so Tom decided to head back to Vail. On the airplane ride back, he cried silently and sorted out his emotions. His world was changing, but he also felt freer from anyone's expectations than he ever had.

21

SPRING

Spring is the time of plans and projects.
—Leo Tolstoy

As March turned into April, several heavy snows dumped on the Vail Valley and then turned into warm early April days. Tom and Eva worked the busy late season and kept looking toward the April 15 closing day of the ski area. The resort's workers lined up summer jobs as rafting guides, restaurant workers, construction workers and a few ski instructors packed their gear to go to the southern Hemisphere, where skiing in Peru and Argentina began their winter.

As closing day drew near the snow thinned and the resort began closing some runs and lifts. On April 15 thousands of people arrived in town and headed up the mountain, where about half of the runs remained open. Atop Chair 4, above mid-Vail, thousands of costumed skiers gathered to party. People in tiger outfits, bikinis and penguin costumes rode the chairlifts and skied. Many then gathered below on Golden Peak for the annual pond skimming competition, where skiers and boarders rode one by one over a jump and into a man-made pond with the goal of skimming across the entire length to the other side. Some flopped fast, others skimmed part way before sinking, and a teen skier did a 360 degree spin off the jump and skimmed across the entire pond to win the contest.

While most other Colorado ski resorts closed in the days after Vail's closing, the highest area Arapahoe Basin planned to stay open until June 5. By May, the usual Spring "freeze-thaw cycle" had set in to create Spring snow conditions. In the cool nights the wet snow froze and created a top layer of ice that greeted skiers when the lifts opened early in the morning. But by 10 a.m. the sun's rays melted the ice and exposed the snow for an acceptable texture between too hard and too soft. But by 1 p.m., the hot sun had melted the snow into a wet slush the skiers called "mashed potatoes" or oatmeal, a sticky mess that posed dangers especially to novice skier because in one moment they could be gliding over partly frozen snow and then hit a wet patch with such sticky resistance that it stops their skis immediately, causing the skier to somersault forward or simply twist a knee severely.

As experienced skiers, Tom and Eva knew they should ski between 10 and 1 p.m. in late season, so one day they headed for Arapahoe Basin for one last day of turns. They arrived in the parking lot to find a large crowd and many people in party mode: tailgates down, grills cooking meats, alcohol being shared, music blaring and dogs running on the snow next to the parking lot. It was called the beach party because the parking lot sat next to the snow and chairlifts, just as a beach sits next to the water. Men in shorts and girls in bikinis enjoyed the warm day and carried their skis and boards to the chairlifts. Tom and Eva shared a drink with a family with an open tailgate and listened to skiers lament the end of the season, but how they looked forward to summer hiking and bicycling and camping.

Tom and Eva took a few runs and talked of this high resort's likely opening the next October, only five months away, when a few runs of man-made snow would open to lure eager skiers, and then Vail would open in November as the next season begins.

They returned home to Vail and stored their ski equipment away for summer. Tom asked Eva and Sophie to come to his house for dinner that night. When they arrived, he asked them to walk a short distance to the covered bridge over the creek so he could show them something before dinner. They walked down to the water by the bridge and Tom reached in his pocket. He took out a tiny lump of metal.

"Remember this?" Tom asked.

Eva nodded yes. "The bullet."

He lifted it up and said "I don't think I need this reminder anymore. I think I've found the people and the place I'm looking for."

He put his arm around Eva and Sophie and hugged them close.

"What about the risks?" Eva said.

"I know. But I don't think you and I are meant to stay on the greens," he said.

And he tossed the bullet in the creek.

Sculpture of skier near Gondola One in Vail Village

CHAPTER NOTES

CHAPTER 1: Regarding courtroom violence, The American Bar Association website reported that Judge Chuck Weller, who was shot in his Reno, Nev. Courthouse, did a study on courtroom violence and "found that court-targeted violence is increasing, even though much money and effort have been put into addressing the issue. Federal courthouses now routinely have weapon-detection systems, surveillance systems and numerous court security officers on guard. Still, incidences of violence —including shootings, bombings and arson attacks — have doubled in the last two decades. Today, Weller writes, there is a violent incident at least once a month in a U.S. courtroom."

CHAPTER 2: Global ski resort statistics from 2016 International Report on Snow and Mountain Tourism, by consultant Laurent Vanat. This report is available for free, to anyone interested at www.vanat.ch.
> US skier statistics from https://www.statista.com/statistics/227427/number-of-skiers-and-snowboarders-usa/.
> The Vail sites and Denver sites heading west on Interstate 70 are factual.
> 26 Colorado ski areas number from https://www.outtherecolorado.com/your-guide-to-all-of-colorados-26-ski-resorts/.

CHAPTER 3: Vail Valley history taken from several sources, including Vail.com. The Vail TV 8 show Good Morning Vail can be watched on the

Comcast network, as of this writing, and online. The driving tour of the Vail Valley sites, including the Wal-mart in Avon, are factual.

CHAPTER 4: Vail arson fires history taken from Vail Daily newspaper. Trail names information from blog.vail.com and other sites.

CHAPTER 5: For good stories on ski bums, see https://unofficialnetworks. com/2012/10/24/society-view-american-ski-bum/ and http:// www.5280.com/2013/11/the-ultimate-guide-to-the-modern-day-ski-bum/. Statistic of helmet usage increase taken from a Vail Daily report. Custom painted helmets are available online. Decimo night-club is a real club, details taken from Vail official information. Story about moonlight skiing near Mt. Hood in Oregon is a true story from a ski instructor friend. Story about night skiing at Matterhorn is taken from the Internet.

CHAPTER 6: History from coloradoski history.com, www.coloradoinfo. com, www.visitsunvalley.com and other sources.

> Vail Resort information from Wikipedia, the Vail Resorts website and https://www.mensjournal.com/features/king-of-the-hill-how-vail-resorts-conquered-the-ski-industry-w469851.

CHAPTER 7: Arapahoe Basin is one of the oldest, highest and most loved ski resorts in Colorado. And one of my favorites. Can't beat the free parking too.

CHAPTER 8: Vail's annual torchlight parade is a real event, reported in many outlets.

CHAPTER 9: Aspen chairlift breakdown is a true story reported in Aspen Daily News and other sources, 2015, although the fictional characters Tom and Eva and their fictional actions are inserted into the real situation. Vail gondola accident and others from varied media sources.

CHAPTER 10: Dog eaten by mountain lion is a true story from Vail Daily newspaper. Children's lesson reference to teaching children to growl is from Parent's Guide to Teaching Skiing, by Paul McCallum and Christine Lariviere McCallum, who mention teaching the tiger roar. Concept of reading skiers by their clothing from an article in meet-mindful.com.

CHAPTER 11: Candide Thovex films on youtube with snow skiing in tunnel and barn is from "One of Those Days 3." The dry skiing video is "Ski the world."

CHAPTER 12: The topic of Mexican immigrants working at ski resort towns has been covered by many media in recent years. One good source for this chapter was a Powder magazine story titled "The Quiet Force." http://www.powder.com/the-quiet-force/#mg2v1ZLfWykzs4SM.99.

CHAPTER 13: Celebrity residents of Vail sourced from www. Accessrealestate.org and Vail magazines. Snow grooming information taken from Litopia, Stevens Pass.com, Utah Adventure Journal, Huffington Post story, and Youtube video called "After Dark with the Breckenridge Grooming Crew."

Ski patrol information from www.breckenridgeskipatrol.com; ski magazine (Ambulance in a Backpack story), SAM magazine (ski area management, sept. 2015 issue, story about patrollers).

CHAPTER 14: Cross-traffic between girlfriends is the enemy of many ski instructors worldwide.

CHAPTER 15: Powder. The pow. Some live for the fluff. Find it when you can. Float the pow.

CHAPTER 16: About ski slang terms, I heard comedian Kevin Nealon on an NPR station one day doing a standup routine and he joked in his material that he went skiing in Colorado but did not yet know that they runs were color coded for difficulty, so when he first asked where the best skiing was, someone told him to watch out for the blacks. They are everywhere. Nealon said he thought the guy was a racist referring to black people. A web search finds several sites that list the many ski slang terms. Some of those sites were purealpine.com, Skipeak.net, Out there monthly.com, and http://mogulmick.vbmco.com/.

CHAPTER 17: Situation of Mexican housekeeping workers being harassed by a supervisor taken from Denver Post article, Feb. 16, 2016. The story reported that a Vail condo company and its parent company were ordered to pay a $1 million settlement to eight undocumented Mexican employees who suffered sexual harassment, discrimination and retaliation when they reported problems to the their bosses. The story said the U.S. Equal Employment Opportunity Commission reported that this was the largest sexual harassment settlement in Colorado history. The story reported that the company's managers were required to attend sexual harassment and discrimination training.

> List of famous politicians and painters from https://news.artnet.com and other sites.

CHAPTER 18: Former ski area information from http://www.colorado-skihistory.com and others.

CHAPTER 19: true stories about instructors falling from lift and losing teeth from former instructor Doug Moen.

CHAPTER 20: Grand Vision story from Vail Daily and Vail Village Homeowners Association, Inc. websites.

CHAPTER 21: Spring skiing is a sweet goodbye to the season. The parties, the friends. Adios amigos.

ABOUT THE AUTHOR

Steve Baska is a former newspaper reporter and editor who lived in Vail, Colorado for one winter season (1978-79) and now lives in the Denver area. He skis each week in winter. For more information on his books, go to **www.stevebaska.com**.

www.ingramcontent.com/pod-product-compliance
Lightning Source LLC
Chambersburg PA
CBHW031317040426
42443CB00005B/102